Praise for *Psyche, Eros, and Me*

Psyche, Eros, and Me weaves Deanna's life as an actress, singer, scholar and woman through the myth of Psyche and Eros. It is a poignant and deeply powerful story. In particular, I enjoyed her approach to the complexity and pertinence of women's issues inherent in this myth, and how the myth of Psyche and Eros continues to connect us to global concerns. A poetic writer, Deanna has a gift for expressing meaning with humor.

—Hendrika de Vries, psychotherapist, author, adjunct professor at Pacifica Graduate Institute

Deanna McKinstry-Edwards' Psyche, Eros, and Me *weaves the story of her soul's search for full blossoming into a rich tapestry. Armed with an artist's equipment, she also has the psychologist's ability to analyze her life choices and ultimately to follow her intuition home to Eros. The myth of Psyche and Eros is her Virgil, the steadfast companion who guides her through the Dark Wood. It is a journey many artists make. As a fellow voyager, my own career benefited from the journey. I only wish I had had Deanna's insights to help straighten out the road.*

—Barbara Babcock, Emmy Award winning actor and author

Deanna McKinstry-Edwards' exhilarating Psyche, Eros, and Me *personalizes the classic myth, making her own story and the myth an immensely entertaining adventure. I found myself immediately drawn into the story, identifying how deeply the quest for Eros has played out in my own life as a woman and an artist. I sense many people will see and find themselves in this treasure trove, and like me, will be unable to put it down until fully read.*

—Melanie Gendron, artist and author of *The Gendron Tarot*, and *This Fool's Journey Through the Tarot's 22 Major Arcana*

Truthfulness, along with the creative craftsmanship to get to the core of experience, always empower important writing. Psyche, Eros, and Me *by Deanna McKinstry-Edwards fulfills both requirements in abundance. Her exploration of the great Greek myth is perfect and thoroughly engaging, as she affirms how we all have to deal with the smoke and mirrors, and—in the words of Dylan Thomas—the "dismays and rainbows" of our own unfolding personal myths as visitors to this existence. Deanna's writing has vitality, depth, and a real freshness. It creates reader-identification and causes ripples in one's own searching thoughts. Her book of going into "the back of the wardrobe" does not just serve her, but also, like all necessary literature, it serves all of us, women and men.*

—Peter Thabit Jones, Welsh poet, author of *The Dylan Thomas Walking Tour of Greenwich Village*

From her New England girlhood to her coming of age at the Pasadena Playhouse, through establishing her career in Hollywood and a whole life beyond, the story of Psyche, Eros, and Me *is Deanna's to be told. Her voice rings clear and true. Deanna has lived Psyche and Eros, and in this book she brings the myth as it may and must be brought forth into the 21st century.*

—John Dotson, poet, playwright, multiple-media artist

Psyche, Eros, and Me

A Mythic Memoir

Deanna McKinstry-Edwards, PhD

Psyche, Eros, and Me
Copyright © 2015 by Deanna McKinstry-Edwards PhD

All rights reserved. No part of this book may be reproduced in any form or by any electronic or mechanical including information storage and retrieval systems, without permission in writing from the author.

ISBN 978-1-935914-63-1

Front cover painting: *He Birthing She* by Carolyn Mary Kleefeld
www.carolynmarykleefeld.com   www.alchemyoracle.com

Back cover photo, cover design and butterfly art by Melanie Gendron
www.gentarot.com

Interior design by River Sanctuary Graphic Arts

Printed in the United States of America

Additional copies available from:
www.riversanctuarypublishing.com
www.Amazon.com

Library of Congress Number: 2015951947

RIVER SANCTUARY PUBLISHING
P.O. Box 1561
Felton, CA 95018
www.riversanctuarypublishing.com
Dedicated to the awakening of the New Earth

CONTENTS

Foreword by Carolyn Mary Kleefeld 1

Introduction: The Myth of Me 3

Prologue 15

The Myth of Psyche and Eros 17

Psyche, Eros, and Me 29

Epilogue: Psyche, Eros—and All of Us 91

Works Cited 106

Acknowledgments 108

FOREWORD

A close friend and colleague recently pointed out that for a work of literature to reach the status of masterpiece it must include the transformation of the main character or characters. In *Psyche, Eros, and Me*, Deanna McKinstry-Edwards skillfully and generously offers this most precious of gifts. Because of the masterful way Deanna braids her fascinating and varied life story into the myth of Psyche and Eros, we may begin to see parallels between our own life stories and this archetypal tale. We are magnetically drawn in, then gently transported from the personal micro to the universal macro as we are led to perceive our own trials and longings for love through this archetypal lens.

In these harshly chaotic times, Deanna's contemporary take on this myth is needed more than ever. As we align our own experiences with Psyche, Eros, and Deanna, somehow our paths become seeded with the flowers of revealing consciousness. The Unknown is not as scary when we can share that reality with others who have triumphantly traversed the wilderness of their own unconscious, who understand how bringing our shadow sides into the light can result in expanded awareness. As we integrate the trials of Psyche and Eros into our own experiences, we may begin to recognize aspects of ourselves asking to be healed and / or transformed, and of our own potential for integrating our humanity with divinity.

We may also come to realize that there is a luminous and omniscient field we can tune into—the world of myth and soul—a resonance we can endeavor to live as a way of life. In the story of Deanna's budding life and her travels with the archetypal wings of poetic symbolism, each of us may also discover visions of our own. We may see that this timeless, mythic zone—the imaginal space between the temporal and the eternal—welcomes us if we so desire. In such an expansive alignment, our individuation can burgeon in newfound ways, with ultimate joy. When ego orientations are shed, we can flourish with enhanced awareness of Source-as-Beloved. In this catalytic work, Deanna radiantly and elegantly presents us with a golden key to transformation.

Bravo, Deanna, for this most essential work.

—*Carolyn Mary Kleefeld*

THE MYTH OF ME

I was born sideways into the world, a breech baby. It seems likely this sideways entrance has shaped me. I know for sure, it scarred me—my forehead retains the dent the forceps bequeathed as they reached inside my mother's womb, turned me around, and pulled me out. My arrival almost brought about my mother's death, when after fifty-six hours of labor an alternate obstetrician intervened. Not for him the Roman Catholic edict of the day declaring that if a baby's delivery was in peril with the life of mother and child in the balance, saving the child's life had the priority. This rescuing doctor chose life for both of us. Who knows how these things happen.

I was born into the icy fingers of an early January morning in Hartford, Connecticut. I was born to a lovely wood and singing stream not too many footsteps from a doorway to the outside world. I was born into arms and hearts with cherishing touches. I was born into the fur of animals—especially that of dogs.

I was born of a woman who wanted children more than anything in life, born into my mother's dream until my own grew wings.

My father loved trains and photographing train wrecks. He smelled of Christmas trees, which he sold—thrilling me to believe he was in league with Santa himself.

I was born into a bootstrap culture—that is, a society of individuals mandated to solve their own problems, whether they had the bootstraps or not.

I was born into a country of John Wayne ideals and heroes, of Walt Disney endings, and of denial.

When I was eight years old, my parents divorced, and the myth of my early life changed dramatically. With no one to help her care for my brother and me, my mother hired a series of women to stay with us while she made her way through various jobs. While my mother worked, my father would occasionally appear, and though he would not exactly kidnap us, he'd take us away for the day without my mother's consent or knowledge of our whereabouts.

To remedy this predicament, my mother made the excruciatingly difficult choice to place my brother and me in the Gilbert Home, an orphanage in Winsted, Connecticut, near Hartford. We two spent several years there, then several more years in foster homes. When I turned thirteen, we were finally reunited with my mother in Boston. Life was still a struggle economically, but she thought I was now sufficiently mature to take care of my brother while she waited tables at night. Our home was a one-room basement apartment on tree-festooned Commonwealth Avenue. While my brother and I watched the legs of the upper world striding by, we ate off the fold-out-of-the wall ironing board that served as our dining table. We played on the stoop of the brownstone where we lived, and we watched television, that wonder of wonders, a late arriving luxury in our lives which we daily adored—until the day it was repossessed. Except for the TV loss, no matter the hardships besetting us, happiness won out. We were together again—at least the three of us.

When we re-formed our household on Commonwealth Avenue, I met my lifelong friend, Melanie Gendron, who had strangely enough just been reunited with her mother after years of being raised by her grandmother. The two of us invented our imaginary dramas and performed them among the echoes of the Boston Public Library ladies' room and in the similarly grand facilities of the Lennox Hotel. While there's no calculating the reasons a young girl may choose to become an actress and a singer, I think such impulses were operating in the background for me even before the big changes caused by my parents' divorce.

I was an imaginative, adventurous, and even mischievous little girl, walking bridge railings, hanging fearlessly from jungle gyms, giving my mom and dad, before their breakup, more than a few palpitations. During the orphanage years, however, the outgoing me met up with a very shy me. The aspirations of the shy me were in conflict with the extravert me. The shy me felt acting would not help save the world, which, in my mind, after our years in the Home, very much needed saving or rescuing. The Home, as you might guess, was far from homey. But all this became the fertile fodder that nourished and molded the actress, singer, and writer and person I would become as my fantasy life effloresced.

I graduated from high school in Cambridge, Massachusetts, and was awarded the Drama Club scholarship. (Believe it or not, I was also Prom Queen. Who *is* she?—I'm sure was the mantra whispered around the gym dance floor. But this is another story.) Next up was Emerson College in Boston, where I received another scholarship. Emerson is noted for both theater and voice therapy, and I chose the latter. The shy me was winning—hoping to save the world one stutterer at a time. One snowy, stormy evening, during the last month of classes, I found myself sitting with other young folks in a spiritual circle at a Unitarian church. Our faces aglow with candlelight, our personal missions, and dreams, we each spoke about what we wanted to do with our lives. As the evening wore on, someone burst into the song "Both Sides Now." Okay, it was I, who hadn't seen either side yet. It was one of those tingly moments when soul stirs and speaks. If you're lucky, you can hear it. I was. I knew I wasn't supposed to be a speech therapist. I was supposed to be singing and acting and reclaiming the vow I made when I wore a peach satin gown as an angel in the Christmas play back at the orphanage.

I got a job and saved enough money to pay for a plane ticket to California for a month-long summer session at the legendary Pasadena Playhouse. Individuals came from around the country to compete for two acting scholarships. I won one, and was then able to attend classes fulltime for two years. Both my mother and father were elated. Their shy daughter had taken a plucky leap and landed on her dreamer's feet.

Although it was nearing the end of its glory days as a fully accredited college/acting mecca, the Pasadena Playhouse inspired every nook and cranny of my being. I lived on one meal a day—don't all fledgling artists? I fell in love with everything that came my way: palm trees (who knew there were so many kinds?), avocadoes (who knew they existed?), mysterious mountains (high, hidden, but becoming visible once the smog lifted), and, of course, love itself.

After finishing the requisite two years of study, I chose to follow a special Boston guy who was a fellow acting student, and I returned to Cambridge where my mother and brother were living. After a period of bi-coastal back-and-forth, my playhouse boyfriend and I drifted apart. A few years later, I met and married Anthony Mauriello, owner of Paul's Mall and the Jazz Workshop, two landmark nightclubs in Boston. Tony also created and ran The Forum, Boston's first *discothèque*. Beautiful women in sexy, short togas served drinks while the records played and bodies writhed nonstop under Greek pillars. Next door, at Ye What Ho, a little pub also owned by Tony, I got a gig singing nightly. I attracted a wee following which followed me to other clubs, including the Playboy Club in Montreal. I opened a few times for headliners at Paul's Mall where the main acts included Flip Wilson, Albert Brooks, Joan Rivers, Bette Midler, Ramsey Lewis, Linda Ronstadt, Barry Manilow, Della Reese, Nina Simone, and John Denver. Next door, the brightest luminaries in jazz filled the lively subterranean chamber of The Jazz Workshop with their scorching artistry—Count Basie, Miles Davis, Charlie Mingus, Errol Garner, Thelonious Monk, Rahsaan Roland Kirk, George Shearing, Bill Evans, Pat Metheny, amongst them.

Tony was a man of integrity, generosity, quiet strength, style, and grace. He and I enjoyed happy years and many travels together. A considerable age difference between us didn't seem to matter, but a lack of similar interests and passions eventually intruded. Plus, it became ever more apparent that there were few opportunities for me to realize my acting and singing dreams in Boston. Once again, I felt something deep within calling me back to Los Angeles, to Hollywood. Born in Boston and having lived there his entire life, Tony was understandably reluctant to leave behind everything he had worked so hard to create. It was a difficult but ultimately friendly parting.

I returned to L.A. with Shanti, my two-year-old golden retriever. We set up base-camp in West Hollywood where I began my rollicking, roller coaster odyssey towards the holy grail of success as an actress. Years of 8x10 photos with changing hair colors and hairdos piled up alongside expanding resumes as I trekked to auditions, landed my acting roles, and played my singing gigs. I waited tables and did typing in offices. For a while, I had a job at the Schick Center for the Control of Smoking where celebrities such as David Niven, Carrie Fisher, and Joan Hackett checked-in nervously for the electrical shocks that they hoped would help them defeat nicotine. I cleaned houses, sang telegrams in mansions and hospitals, and then drove away in my broken down VW Beatle. I sang in restaurants that featured singing waitresses. One minute I'd be belting "The Long and Winding Road," the next I'd be plopping down a plate of ribs. For several months I worked at the Improvisation nightclub, a hallowed shrine for aspiring comics. There, during the golden years, Robin Williams, David Letterman, Jay Leno, Richard Lewis, Freddie Prinze, and countless others polished and presented their talents in hopes of getting a spot on Carson or Merv Griffin—which often launched their careers.

The reviews from my first play, *Mustard*, staged at the Matrix Theater in Hollywood, were stellar. "Deanna McKinstry steals the show in two musical numbers, 'I'm Naïve' and 'Big City Blues' . . . Ms. McKinstry has *star* written all over her." A funny fella and wonderful actor also in the play was Steve Moore. Steve and I became close friends, and when the play ended, we plotted ways to make money to pay the rent till stardom kicked in. *Voilà!* We created a ragtag musical comedy act, *Beauty and the Burger*, later called *McKinstry and Moore*. We sang, did jokes, performed a skit on *The Gong Show* that paid us scale and also won us an answering machine, our first. Audiences loved our chemistry and antics, loved my singing. Though not destined or intended for greatness, our odd mishmash of an act did at times pay the rent.

That's how it goes in Hollywood, a place more akin to a mythic kingdom than an actual spot on a map. One is not only grateful for any job that can provide room and board, one builds up a repertoire of job-experience anecdotes about the trials and tribulations encountered upon the yellow brick road to Oz-dom. No one can top an actor's stories at a dinner party except maybe another actor. After all, one must have *something* witty to say on Leno or Letterman when the Big Turning Point of one's career arrives. Yes, aspiring actors/performers live on the fuel of hopes while tooling around in beat-up cars with gas gauges on Empty. It's all part of living the dream.

As fortune had it, I looked quite a bit younger than my age, and although many friends were younger than me, some thought I was younger than them. Naturally, being in the business, I lied or withheld the truth all the time. At auditions, an actor/actress isn't usually asked her/his age; she or he auditions for a role in a certain age range. For instance, the producers are looking for a woman twenty-five to thirty-three, and it's your perceived age that matters. This keeps many of us very young for a very long time. It's the Hollywood math. In truth, in "real life" I was quite naïve, and decidedly younger in spirit than my biological age. Meaning, the gazillion experiences that shaped those years of my life were seen through the eyes of a very optimistic, enthusiastic young woman with very thick lenses in her rose-colored glasses.

In looking back, certain experiences that I had stand out as iconic. They represent some of the more clichéd ideas about *life upon the wicked stage,* as the song goes. One of these typified the orgiastic stories that the Hollywood Hills inspire. One night, after performing in a play I was doing, a fellow actor invited me to dinner at the house of his friend. The friend was Hugh Hefner. The house was The Mansion. The actor/date was formerly a child star on a highly successful TV western, a lovely fellow, somewhat shy. Once we found a parking space amongst the circus of cars surrounding The Mansion, I followed him through the throngs— it could have been hundreds—who had also come for "dinner with a friend." The occasion was a celebration of Hefner's latest breakup. After being introduced to Hef and downing a few drinks—alcohol for him, fruit juice for me—my date became somewhat *other* than his customary self.

His heroes, he told me, were John Wayne, and Hefner. And in fact, the more he drank, the more I could see John Wayne and Hefner struggling to emerge in him. Still respectful and sweet, he led me down to an underground grotto where he suggested we take a swim with countless, naked others. I declined, but feeling out of place, and having zero idea of where to go, I followed him to poolside where couples were engaged in various stages of love-making, i.e., performing sexual acts. "Oh, thank you!" I smiled, "Hi there, nice to see you!" You don't get much more Dionysian than that, at least for a girl from Boston, where members of the African ballet company were required to put on bras. Even then, I thought how romantic this ambiance might be—if only it weren't Hugh Hefner's place with hundreds of people. Funny how that is.

In those earliest of my Hollywood years, I was as much as anything singing and pursuing my career as a recording artist. While I had been married to Tony, I'd written quite a few songs that I had on tape and shopped around town. I made a bad decision early on with a well-known manager, with whom I unwittingly signed over songs without writing into the contract a time frame for returning the rights to me. That was a hard lesson and a valuable one. But within the first year, I also met Mario Padilla, a beautiful fella who wanted to record me. A talented musician-composer, he took me into the studio where I recorded several of my songs and a couple of his. Mario shopped the demo tape around, but with few connections in the music biz, alas, the few nibbles never manifested into a recording contract. Nonetheless, Mario did arrange for me to sing on *The Dinah Shore Show*. He and I still love to talk about those struggling but cherishable moments of our salad days. He's now a PhD professor of English. One of his children now studies voice with my husband.

The years glimmered by for this *glimmering girl* where success and disappointments merged into a mostly happy leaping towards my dreams. I performed in plays in L.A. theaters, doing comedies, musical comedies, and tragedies. I did guest roles on TV soaps and sit-coms. In feature films, I had a few teensy roles that were cut or never made the light of day. I did commercials and voice-overs, and sang in nightclubs and coffee houses.

I sang in demos for composers hoping to sell their songs to established artists, including singing the theme song for a couple of TV shows.

Several times during the years of living on the edges of economic disaster, I was set for my major breakthrough. I felt it. Those around me were sure of it. Most actors have a few close calls with pending big-time success. One of the most entrancing moments was auditioning for *Marilyn*, a Broadway-bound musical based on the life of Marilyn Monroe. Looking at me at the time, you would not have thought I was a perfect candidate—too thin, kind of angular, not a big enough bra size. But a dear friend, John Carlyle, who later mentioned me in his Hollywood memoir, *Under the Rainbow*, was convinced the producers were looking for a particular quality—Vulnerability—and that he saw in me. As it turned out, he was right. After the auditions, I was the frontrunner in L.A. for the starring role. In the months that followed, countless ups and downs rocked the *Marilyn* production. When I didn't hear from them, I auditioned for and was cast in *Last Lucid Moment*, a play directed by Jon Voight.

One propitious night a call came from New York. *Marilyn* was in rehearsals, but the new producers wanted to recast the lead. They wanted me to fly to NYC immediately to re-audition. I was opening the very next night in Jon's play, and there was no stand in for me. No way on Earth would I have left him in the lurch, especially as some hinky things had already occurred with the Marilyn production. "Besides," Jon advised, "don't feel you always have to jump when they say so." Long story short, *Marilyn* opened and closed in less than a week—without me. Working with Jon, a brilliant, perceptive director and a lovely man, was one of the best experiences of my acting life.

Among my earliest plays in L.A., produced at the award-winning Odyssey Theater in Santa Monica, was a piece that also hadn't made it on Broadway. Like many similarly "failed" Broadway shows, it found its way to a smaller theater. *Something's Rockin' in Denmark* was a rock opera based on Bill Shakespeare's acclaimed play, *Hamlet*. I played Gertrude. Strong singers, and a smart, innovative director, Dan Castilleno, turned this rock opera into a rave production. One day during rehearsals, when we actors were struggling with our *recitative,* Dan said something that settled into me so deeply that I wrote about it many years later in my dissertation. "I can't tell you how to do this," he said with his customary passion, "but each one of you has to find why it is you're singing the phrase you're singing rather than speaking it. This is epic stuff, everybody—mythic to its core."

In the production of *Something's Rockin',* I met a lovely, talented actress and singer who became one of my closest friends, Patricia Gaul. Some years later, I worked with Patricia writing plays and organizing fundraisers for the Los Angeles Children's Theater, which she founded.

Near the end of my fifth year in Hollywood, I landed an astonishingly lucrative job in Reno headlining a car show extravaganza at the MGM Grand Hotel, which then had the largest stage in the world—big enough, in fact, for an actual airplane with chorus girls on its wings to be wheeled on stage as I regaled the audience with the virtues of American Motor's cars. At this event, I met the elegant and witty John Carlyle, my lifelong friend, mentioned above. With the payoff from this gig, I had funds to take singing lessons with an L.A. voice teacher, Robert Edwards, about whom I had heard. He'd heard about me too, through mutual friends.

Rob's telling of our meeting is much more romantic, sure to bring a tear to the eye, than my own. He had already heard me sing on a tape that a client of his had brought to his studio. He was rather "in love" with my voice. My memory of that first lesson is of my unintentionally spitting on him, while trying to do an exercise I couldn't do. Even so, I left that first lesson on a cloud, feeling intuitively that I'd met someone who would take my voice to a whole new level. That he did. However, destiny had a great deal more in store for us.

Rob had a beard, a mustache, and long hair, all the accoutrements of the 60s including a two-toned, blue VW camper, his pride and joy. This was, however, the 80s. We dated for almost four years, taking trips with Shanti through Northern California and the Southwest with his pride and joy often terrifying me as it lurched down canyons and mountains, and barely crawled up canyons and mountains. With no air-conditioning,

Rob's *pride and joy* gave Dante's Inferno a run for its money. We had to shout out above the engine noise to hear each other talk. When the vehicle was still, however, the camper was a veritable love nest on wheels, great for traveling with Shanti and having our wild kingdom adventures.

Having both become devotees of Paramahansa Yogananda, we chose to be married in the little Wind Mill Chapel, beautifully situated by a small lake in the middle of the grounds of the Self Realization Fellowship Temple in Pacific Palisades. During the years that followed, Robert's teaching exploded into a spectacularly successful career. At his vocal studio in Sherman Oaks, Rob has taught some of the most talented and well-known singers of the present day—Christina Aguilera, Sheryl Crowe, Linda Ronstadt, Bonnie Raitt, Tracey Chapman, to name a few. Rob's vocal expertise is only part of the key to his success. The personal attention that he gives to each of his clients enriches and often changes their lives. Eventually, we were fortunate enough to buy a home in the Hollywood Hills and thanked our lucky stars for the wildlife, deer, coyote, hawks, and raccoons outside our door.

I continued to act, sing, and perform some of the best roles of my life. As time went by, however, finding good roles was challenging. Well-written parts for actresses diminish as they age—a cliché, but years ago a real and distressing one. To a significant degree this remains so. Not only do roles for mature actresses vanish, it's almost as if women, and especially actresses, also disappear. Many women talk about their becoming invisible at this time.

Not wanting to wait around for the phone to ring, I became interested in the predicament of mature actresses, as it was beginning to happen to me. I wrote a novel about it, a fictional memoir/novel called *She Who Vanishes*. It also occurred to me that if there were a group of women who would have some wisdom about this mid-life vanishing act, it might be actresses older than me. In fact, the big stars of yesterday might be thriving and doing other things with their lives. To this end, I decided to interview as many of the glorious women actresses of the past as I could find and get access to. I hoped to find out what they were doing. I tentatively called my book of interviews, *The Disappearance of Once Highly Visible Women*.

I interviewed several movie stars—the late Janet Leigh, whose new love was writing. The late Patricia Neal, who still acted occasionally and continuously embraced life with grace and zest. Tippi Hedren took her love for animals and created a wildlife animal preserve, Shambhala, which rescues tigers, lions, big cats, even an elephant. Rhonda Fleming's energies were channeled into a medical center in honor of her late sister who had died of cancer. Rita Gam also became a writer, and like all the above women was still stunning and living life to the full. This project came to an end when I went back to school and began the long road of caretaking my ailing mother.

But before that happened, I'd also written a couple of screenplays. One, optioned several times, centered on a whimsical story wherein a Native American wins a national lottery that has been created to help defray the national debt. The winner as it turns out would rather get back the Black Hills than take any money. I was deeply fascinated by Indian lives, histories, philosophies, and mythologies. Interested in my script, Russell Means, the well-known American Indian Movement activist, fresh off his movie success in *The Last of the Mohicans*, came over one night for dinner. Ultimately, the right connections and financing eluded the project. File under Another Close Call.

As acting opportunities dwindled, the writing increased. I wrote for magazines, and I interviewed concerned individuals like Deepak Chopra, John Robbins, director Michael Apted, and actor Ed Begley. For a short while I was an assistant editor for a newsletter distributed by *Actresses@ Work*, an organization aiming to enhance roles for older actresses by reflecting more authentically the lives of mature women.

My biological clock was ticking loudly, and I was working to establish why I wasn't getting pregnant—when my mother had a massive stroke. Bereft of speech and facing a life of living alone back in Massachusetts, I brought her to Los Angeles, to be near Robert and me.

And so it was that stirrings to follow a different drummer came upon me. My soul was speaking up again, and I *listened*, just as I had long before at the Unitarian church in Boston. The myth of my life was soon to take me far afield from where I had lived and breathed and had my being, into the novel and stimulating territory of mythology and depth psychology. As the twentieth century sounded its crescendo into the twenty-first century, I began an extraordinary and transforming odyssey to return to school. There, in 1999, at the crossroads of the-me-I-was and the-me-I-would-become, I met the myth of Psyche and Eros.

PROLOGUE

This is a tale that needs be told. For heartache and broken dreams roam the land yearning for that which sweetens and that which mends. From these lamentations Eros is rising, in raiment not dimmed by forgetfulness, banishment, or by time. For Eros knows what only Eros bestows—that love is not a mere moment among mortals. It is *the* moment we live for! It is sacred energy generating life into more life. It is the heart of the Universe wedding spirit to flesh, when the fires of transformation are kindled. Eros bedews the body with radiance divine. Eros lights the world even unto its darkest realms. But the story is not so simple.

This is an old tale. Indeed, it is the human story, and the story prior to humans and nonhumans appearing on earth. We have journeyed far from the chaos and tempestuous music of our beginnings. What we were once upon a time remains part of who we've become and who we might become. Then, as now, our creature-hood needs the flames and moisture that Eros bestows, arousing us body and soul to a wholeness that enlivens our intimacies with one another, and with the natural world we are a part of. Today we are being summoned to awaken to the erotic world we live in. An ally of Eros, Zephyrus, the West Wind, has heard our supplications and rushes towards us with his pinions wide and tipped in gold—the gold of transformation.

This is the story of Psyche and how she finally found what she wanted most…her Beloved Eros, and her deepest, fullest, authentic Self.

—*Deanna McKinstry-Edwards, PhD*

THE MYTH OF PSYCHE AND EROS

. . . an imaginative telling based on the tale by Apuleius

In Western Greece, in a time not so long ago, a king and queen lived with their three beautiful daughters. When two of them came of age, they swiftly found quite resplendent and immensely wealthy princes to marry. But the third, the youngest, was most beautiful of all—hers was another story. There were words to describe the attractiveness of the older sisters, but there were no words to describe the youngest sister's extraordinary beauty. Men found her sensually alluring, yet an otherworldly quality set her apart. She possessed both a lush sexuality not often encountered and a radiance of spirit not often seen. Men were more likely to worship Psyche rather than to love her as a flesh and blood woman.

Word of her femininity traveled far into the world. Wherever she went, Psyche was surrounded by adoring followers, many of whom came from distant lands to gaze upon her. Admiring throngs followed her everywhere even when she entered the temple to offer her deepest devotion to the Great Goddess of them all, Aphrodite, Queen of Love and Beauty. Garlands of flowers and gifts once laid at Aphrodite's feet were now heaped upon Psyche. No matter where she went, she could not escape the adulation and awe of her admirers.

"We have discovered a new Aphrodite, a new goddess, a goddess born of the dew of the earth, not the dew of the ocean," the crowds clamored, and with all their ardor directed toward Psyche, the ashes of remembrance on the altars of Aphrodite turned sodden with neglect. It was unimaginable that anyone could displace the glorious Goddess of Love from the hearts of mortals, and indeed, this cooling of allegiance drove a stake into Aphrodite's heart and unleashed her fury. "How shall a girl, a child of the earth, doomed to die, parade in my likeness?" she raged, as black revenge rumbled from her primordial depths.

From that moment, the great Goddess set about to destroy Psyche, who was in no way responsible for what had befallen her. The goddess was well within her means, for it was She who knew and bestowed love in all its many guises. Those She ravished with her oceanic powers rose up like her beautiful doves to ecstatic heights of feeling and being. When She withheld herself, life in all its sweetness withered away. With womanly desires only faintly beginning to stir within her, Psyche was no match for the Goddess. Knowing this well, Aphrodite plotted her avengement with Olympian delight.

Meanwhile, Psyche's father, the king, and her mother, the queen, began to suspect that their daughter's difficulty in finding a suitable husband might be attributable to Aphrodite's resentment. Determined to appease the Goddess, the royal parents contacted the Oracle at Delphi for advice. The Oracle's response left no doubt, indeed, about the divine discontent. Hoping to rectify the situation, Psyche's parents beseeched the Oracle to tell them what to do. They received a startling and deeply distressing answer.

"O king, you are to bring your daughter to the mountaintop. Dress her in funereal robes to meet her spouse. A bridegroom he is, not of mortal seed, but rather a wingéd creature fierce and cruel."

Sadness beyond words filled the hearts of Psyche's parents on hearing this torturous pronouncement rendered upon their precious daughter's future and destiny. But fearing, as most mortals did, disastrous retribution from the Great Goddess they saw no alternative but to do her bidding. Oracles were not to be questioned.

Grief stricken to their core and with much weeping, the king and queen dressed their beautiful Psyche in the finest wedding finery. When night came, those forming the torch-lit wedding procession, more like a funeral, wound their way to the top of the mountain. With hearts sinking and hands shaking, they did as they were told to do, chained their beloved Psyche on a rocky outcrop, and departed.

As the few remaining torches were extinguished, Psyche waited, terrified and alone in the bone-chilling cold and darkness of night. She knew the one Aphrodite had picked to be her husband was the ugliest, most horrifying monster, Thanatos, lord of death. As Psyche shivered with dread and exhaustion, Aphrodite dispatched her magnificent son, Eros, the god of love, to go to the mountain and shoot a gold-pointed arrow into Psyche, thus to ensure her falling deeply in love with the monster selected to be her husband. Even the deities, with all their powers, were not exempt from Eros's potent arrows that compelled those so pricked to fall in love with the very first person seen afterward. More than happy to carry out this mission at the behest of his mother, Eros flew straightaway to the mountaintop. But what he saw undid him. Psyche's beauty and vulnerability so captured his nature that he forgot what task he was there to accomplish. As he alighted beside Psyche, his soft white wings brushed tenderly across her face. Overcome with emotion, he began to make love to her, and doing so, he accidentally pricked himself with one of his own gold-pointed arrows and fell completely in love with her.

In that moment, Psyche experienced feelings that she had never before felt in her body. The mountain, the cold, and the stars dissolved into streams of pleasure rushing over her skin and through her flesh. As her body moved and opened to the touch of Eros, sounds rose out of her to fill the darkness, sounds she had never made before. She was liquid and soft, endlessly pliable. She hardly knew where her body ended and her lover's began.

When their lovemaking was over, Eros knew he wanted Psyche for himself. He called upon his friend Zephyrus, the West Wind, and asked him to gently lift and deliver his beloved down into his personal paradise, a valley of otherworldly splendor.

When Psyche awoke following their lovemaking, Eros was gone. As it was still night, and sensing someone else was near, she trembled. Was this the monster with the hideous talons of her destiny? It certainly didn't feel that way. Instead the silky, sheltering wings of the West Wind swept her up and carried her like a leaf down into a verdant valley. Zephyrus laid her on soft moonlit grasses and wildflowers. There she fell into a deep sleep until morning.

At dawn when Psyche awakened she found herself by a lush grove of trees. Through these she could make out the contours of a most noble residence. Emboldened by the beauty of the valley glistening with sunshine, she took it upon herself to see the great house up close. Hesitantly she entered. It was the most magnificent structure she had ever seen. It was fashioned from the finest woods and metals, gilded in gold, and bedecked with the most exquisite jewels and tiles imaginable. As she walked about the rooms, invisible fairy-like voices welcomed her in friendly tones.

A huge feast was laid at a long banquet table with only one chair. Exceeding hungry, Psyche sat down and ate heartily, serenaded by a single voice accompanied by a lyre. Twilight soon blurred the sky mango and carnelian. A cool breeze ruffled the silk curtains as darkness fell. Psyche heard footsteps. Her heart leapt with trepidation. Could this be the monster bridegroom? Then she heard a deep voice, irresistibly masculine, and sweet as honey.

"Do not be alarmed, beautiful Psyche. It is my wish that this house and all that dwells within it are yours if you will be my bride. All that I ask of you is that you obey my command. I will spend every night with you. We will travel to the stars and back again with pleasure. But each morning, before dawn, I will fly away. You must never ask to see my face or to know who I am. Trust me, and I promise you, we will be happy beyond the ends of time."

And then the strong, stirring arms of the one who had earlier touched her as no one had ever touched her reached for her again and held her close, smoothing away her anxieties. In the embrace of Eros, Psyche felt the sublime spirit of manly desire and love, and she knew it was to be sought out and relished for its elixir of rapture and divinity.

Night after night Eros came to Psyche and filled her with his love until every particle in her body and soul knew the shapes, the sounds, the taste and touch of his body. "I wonder who you are," Psyche whispered, "but even though I can't see you, I love you as I love life."

However, as the days went by, something stirred in Psyche. Sometimes when night fell and she heard her lover's wings, a peculiar anguish filled her. How she longed to see his face, to know him in the light of day, to see his eyes in the sunlight and the color of the curls that framed the soft skin of his face. She was most grateful for the life she had, but a deep yearning was mounting within her.

While gathering roses one day, and now pregnant, Psyche heard news that her sisters were grief-stricken by her death. How she missed sharing with them her wonderful life and the news of the child growing within her. She was moved to pity for their concern and wanted them to know she was very much alive. When Eros came to her that night, she asked him if she could see her sisters to share her good fortune and relieve their mourning. Reluctantly, Eros agreed—but reminded Psyche that she must not tell her sisters anything about him or their life together.

What joy Psyche felt the very next day when Zephyrus ushered the two sisters down into her garden. When they first arrived, they were filled with relief and exulted that Psyche was well and happy. As they heard more of the extent of Psyche's august wealth and circumstances, including the husband she adored, their feelings turned dark-hearted. In Psyche's enthusiasm to share her good fortune, she was blinded to the treacherous jealousy tearing through her sisters' hearts. Neither of them was married to a man she loved. One was married to an older ailing man who treated her as a daughter, and the other married to a crippled man who needed to be mothered. Certainly, they wanted not for material things, but they saw in Psyche's demeanor a woman lifted to great heights by the man she loved. When the sisters asked for particulars about this man, Psyche grew oddly evasive. The sisters grew suspicious, and their feelings turned increasingly traitorous. Alarmed by their inquiries, the nearby Zephyrus, who had the best interests of Eros at heart, took the situation upon himself and whisked the sisters back to their homes.

When Psyche recounted their visit to Eros, he sensed disaster in the making. He knew the sisters would press Psyche to know as much about him as possible, and in truth, their conversations kindled a longing in

Psyche to see them again. She had become frustrated by a life that required little of her. She tired of flower arranging and repeating the same activities day after day. She tired of laying out fine fabrics for dresses to be made, tired of her needlepoint, tired of picking roses.

Once again, reluctantly, Eros agreed to a visit, but he told Psyche that if things went wrong, a serious reversal of circumstances would threaten the life they were living together, and also destroy the fortunes of the child they had conceived together—who would not be born as a divine child but as a mere mortal.

The bitter sisters had in fact hatched a malevolent plan. They told Psyche that the neighbors had reported seeing a hideous, winged serpent flying into the valley. Planting alarming doubts in Psyche's unsuspecting mind, they implored her not to be deceived, for it was rumored that after the birth of her baby the monster would spring forth to devour both child and mother.

Gravely disturbed, Psyche protested, but the sisters knew their scheme had been effective, that it had raised doubts in Psyche's mind. Dripping with false concerns and kindness, they urged Psyche to follow their instructions.

"Tonight when your lover falls asleep, take a sharp knife, and with a lighted lamp take a good look. If what we say is true, cut off his head and save your life and that of your child," and then they departed.

Alone, Psyche's fears and doubts assailed her with all the whys for which she had no answers. Why did her husband insist on their joining in darkness? Why did he not share what he did all day while he was away? Why did he come to her only at night? Why was he so vehemently against her sisters' visits?

As her misgivings mounted into panic, Psyche increasingly felt that she had to gain at least a glimpse of her beloved husband's face. Finally one night, with a courage she didn't know she had, she prepared to do exactly as her sisters told her and to disobey Eros.

That evening after their lovemaking, when Eros fell asleep, Psyche was ready. Rising, she took up the whetted knife in one hand and the lamp in the other. Then she returned to their warm bed and quietly lit the lamp. She lifted it over the body of her gentle Eros. So stunned was she at what she saw, she nearly collapsed. Below her was the most exquisite looking male she had ever seen, his smoothly muscled body draped in stirring splendor upon the sheets. Thick ebony curls clustered around his sweet, trusting face. His lips, moist as raspberries, parted gently. Her heart rang with his beauty. As she bent to kiss his divine forehead, a drop of hot oil sputtered from the lamp and fell onto his shoulder.

Startled awake, Eros saw Psyche standing over him with knife in hand. Instantly, he darted from the bed. Immediately comprehending the sisters' deceitfulness, and shooting a scalding look back at Psyche, Eros sprang towards the window. Not knowing what else to do, Psyche grabbed his foot and held on as he flew out the window and high into the night sky—toward his home and mother Aphrodite.

Holding on for dear life, Psyche soon grew tired, lost her grip, and fell back to earth. The palace and all its treasures had vanished. She was utterly alone on a deserted plain. With nowhere to go and no one to go to, she was consumed by unbearable loss and sadness. Her sobs could be heard for miles. She was no longer wife to her beloved.

Gripped with wretchedness, Psyche decided to go to the river and throw herself in. When she did so, the river spat her out, refusing to take her in. Then she encountered the cloven-footed god Pan. Sensing her plight, he played on his flute to distract and deter her from committing more harm to herself. He told her that the best thing she could do was to pray. And so she did, invoking all the gods and goddesses with supplication. Though they felt compassion for Psyche, the divinities knew better than to interfere in the affairs of the great Aphrodite, and they all declined to help.

At wit's end, and with nowhere else to turn, Psyche decided to approach Aphrodite and to throw herself on her mercy, hoping that for love's sake, the goddess might take pity. This was not to be. With barely a foot in the temple door, Psyche realized she was not going to be let off the hook. In a withering tirade, Aphrodite called Psyche every demeaning name in the book—a low-life, good-for-nothing nobody. Psyche took it all and never flinched. Her tirade subsiding, Aphrodite then paused for effect and offered Psyche a deal—*The Deal*. If Psyche could complete four do-or-die tasks, she would be spared death and reunited with Eros. Knowing that a mere mortal could never accomplish the tasks, Aphrodite was certain that Psyche's fate was sealed.

The first task involved sorting a huge mound of seeds, flax, wheat, barley, millet, rye, and bulgur heaped together in a mishmash—food for the doves that pulled Aphrodite's golden and bejeweled chariot. "Take these, and grain by grain separate them by kind into their own piles by nightfall," ordered Aphrodite, and off she flew in her glittering transport.

Psyche gazed at the heap of seeds, and with each sigh, her resolve melted at the enormity of the task. Seconds later, an ant skittered out from under a rock, and moved by Psyche's predicament, summoned hundreds of other ants. They made quick work, and by nightfall they had sorted the seeds. For the first time since Eros left her, Psyche felt something like hope.

When Aphrodite returned at day's end, she was not pleased. With her customary arrogance, she threw Psyche a crust of bread for her efforts and told her that tomorrow she would face an even more difficult task. A weary Psyche fell asleep upon the hard ground.

The next morning Aphrodite issued her second demand, a task of heightened difficulty. "On the opposite shore of that river stand some rams. Bring me their golden fleece by day's end."

As before, the task seemed beyond Psyche's endurance. The rams were known for their fierceness. Overwhelmed, Psyche headed for the riverbank to drown herself for sure this time. As she knelt by the river's edge, the slim green reeds whispered to her, "Psyche, you must avoid the rams in the noonday sun when they are most active. Wait until evening when the river has cooled them and they are lulled to sleep. Then you can cross over and pick their golden wool off the brambles they brushed against during the day."

This Psyche did. She waited until the sun turned its face away, and when the rams settled into their evening sleep, she swam across the river and easily picked their golden fleece off the bushes until her arms were full.

The sight of Psyche loaded down with golden fleece sent Aphrodite into a whirling rage. "You will not outwit me with this third task," she fumed. "Take this crystal vessel and fill it with the waters from the Fountain of Forgetfulness."

The Fountain of Forgetfulness, along with its twin, The Fountain of Remembrance, gushed from a hidden crevasse high atop a mountain that no mortal had ever climbed. Where the two streams converged below was the River of Life. On either side of this river were two caves, both inhabited by deadly monsters.

Gazing to the heights, Psyche knew she could never make it to the summit. Even the river as it rushed past shouted at her to flee for her life. The timing, however, was right for a supportive thread of synchronicity. Zeus, disgusted with Aphrodite's continual uproars and jealousies, had grown sensitive to Psyche's situation, and he sent his eagle that could fly higher than any bird to help her.

At the very edge of despair, Psyche heard the powerful whooshing of the eagle's wings dipping low and welcoming her to climb aboard his back. Soaring to the high hidden crevasse, the eagle flew close to where the waters streamed forth from the Fountain of Forgetfulness. Psyche promptly filled the crystal vessel.

The task completed, the eagle deposited Psyche gently back on the ground. Bearing the healing waters, Psyche bounded joyfully down the mountainside. Pleased again at her success, she entered Aphrodite's chamber. The Queen of Love was far from delighted. With determination furiously intensified, Aphrodite decreed a fourth task, a most formidable task, one that the goddess knew was utterly impossible for Psyche to complete.

She handed Psyche a small pot with a lid and told her that she must visit Persephone in the Underworld and bring back some of her immortal beauty ointment. Most importantly, Psyche must deliver this pot to

Aphrodite unopened. Psyche knew this was surely the end. Distraught and despairing of ever seeing her beloved Eros again, Psyche took herself to a Tower to jump off. When she ascended to the top, she was stopped cold by the very stones beneath her feet—they spoke to her.

"No, Psyche, do not do this. There is a way to fulfill this task and live. You must follow a path tangled with thorns from yonder cave. It leads down to the Underworld. Put two coins in your mouth and take two pieces of barley bread in your hands, then follow the path. When you come to a lame donkey and a lame driver who will ask you to pick up some sticks, pass him by. When you come to the River Styx, use one of your coins to pay Charon to row you across. Further on, you must refuse the groping hand of a dying man as he reaches out of the water begging you to save him. When you encounter three women weaving the threads of fate and fantasy, be on your way without stopping to talk with them. When you reach the entrance to hell, toss one of your pieces of barley bread to Cerberus, the three-headed dog that stands guard. While the three heads are fighting over the one piece of bread, enter the Palace of Hades where Persephone is queen. She will give you a portion of her immortal beauty ointment. Put it into the pot with the tight fitting lid. Repeat the whole process on your way back up. And remember, you must deliver the pot unopened."

Hope kindled Psyche's heart once more. It seemed possible that she and Eros might be together again. She scrupulously followed the advice of the Tower. One mistake could be her undoing. She procured the ointment and returned safely from the Underworld. All that remained was to deliver the unopened pot to Aphrodite, and then she would be with the one who moved her spirit towards its most radiant aliveness. But as she walked along, she caught her reflection in the river. She now looked haggard, her once beautiful face now deeply creased by her life-and-death struggles.

Desiring to feel beautiful again, Psyche opened the pot and took a little of the immortal beauty ointment for herself. Instantly, a strange vapor from the pot overpowered her, and she fell into a deathly sleep. Hearing the sound of her falling, Eros flew to her as fast as his wings could carry him. He shook her, "Psyche, Psyche, my beloved, wake up. Your curiosity has almost ruined you again. But I am here. All things are possible. Our love can surmount the mightiest obstacles."

The pot was brought to Aphrodite without her knowing the whole story. Pleading his case to Zeus and the gods in the days that followed, Eros proposed that his beloved mortal wife be made immortal. His wish was granted.

During the celebrative feast, with all the gods and goddesses in attendance, Zeus handed Psyche the cup of immortality. Before she drank, Psyche looked over at Aphrodite, whose beauty outshined all the other goddesses. Tears decorated her cheeks like dewy primroses. And in that moment, Psyche understood that what endures in this world are the strengths of the gifts of the Great Goddess of Love. Psyche's human tears mirrored those of Aphrodite, and they smiled at one another, knowingly.

As Psyche brought the cup and nectar of immortality to her lips and drank, two butterfly wings sprouted from her shoulders. Even though Psyche became immortal, she remained forever human. When she and Eros were joined in their human-divine marriage and the stars spangled the sky of celebration, Aphrodite danced and danced all through the night, for she knew she had helped bring a new kind of love into the world.

Out of the love between Psyche and Eros, a child named Pleasure—sometimes called Joy or Voluptas—was born. Even before she was born, Pleasure knew in the deepest depths that her body and spirit were one. She had inherited the legacy of Psyche's difficult journey. Pleasure knew she was both human and divine.

PSYCHE, EROS, AND ME

Sometimes a person needs a story more than food to stay alive.
—Barry Lopez, *Crow and Weasel*

The story of Psyche and Eros entered my life when I needed it. Perhaps stories arrive when a yearning for them reaches a certain pitch. Certainly this seemed to be the case with my meeting the story of Psyche and Eros.

I had known the words *psyche* and *eros* for a good many years and entertained some idea of their meanings and manifestations in my life. The word psyche is often used interchangeably to mean mind, self, and most especially, soul. Eros is the god of love, love itself, although often construed to be sexual love exclusively. I also knew, though vaguely, that there is a Greek myth about Psyche and Eros. Then one blustery bright spring day some years ago in Carmel, California, a friend suggested a book on Psyche and Eros, one that I immediately sought and bought. From the first page, I began an exhilarating personal journey with these two mythic beings that granted me wings towards new dreams, new directions, and a deepening sense of self and personal sovereignty.

The first written rendition of the tale of Psyche and Eros appears in the second century Latin novel *The Golden Ass* by Lucius Apuleius. The myth is retold in *Amor and Psyche, the Psychic Development of the Feminine* by Erich Neumann, a disciple of C.G. Jung, and himself among the most distinguished analytical psychologists of his time. Though separated by many centuries and living within patriarchal worldviews, both Apuleius and Neumann, male storytellers, were keenly interested in and quickened by the landscape of the feminine. Apuleius was a student of the Eleusinian Mysteries. Although these rites had disappeared before his lifetime, they had flourished for thousands of years in the life-world of the Great Mother societies. Neumann wrote of Apuleius that "he was one of those creative men, who like the feminine, must give birth, one of those whom Psyche guides." The same might be said of Neumann, the difference being he explored feminine sensibilities through Jungian psychology and the lens of archetypes and symbolism.

Jungian psychology entered my life during my twenties via *Knowing Woman* by Irene Claremont de Castillejo. A strong wind blasting open creaky windows, this book stirred inner realms that I barely understood at the time. Over the years, I have never forgotten it. This was my first venture into the depths of the archetypes.

Archetypes are the handmaidens of Jungian analysis and therapy. When an archetype is at work in one's life—and that's *all* the time—a Jungian therapist can help name it and provide a map of the behaviors and conditions it may be activating. Several thousand years of patriarchy have created a history of unspeakable heartache and madness by eclipsing and exterminating our feminine capacities for relatedness and holistic thinking. Living life predominantly from one side of our brains, the left side, has cast long shadows of *dis*-ease. A Jungian understanding of archetypes can be helpful in reclaiming and re-enlivening the muffled or extinguished qualities of our feminine nature. Jungian perspectives emphasize balancing masculine and feminine energies within each of us.

Among my favorites of several inspiring and illuminating tellings of the tale of Psyche and Eros are Jean Houston's *Search For the Beloved* and Diana Wolkstein's *The First Love Stories*. Mary Hugh Scott's *The Passion of Being Woman* focuses on a Psyche set free from the destructive effects patriarchy has exacted upon the life of Eros. Scott evokes the primal, indigenous voice of the feminine prior to patriarchal influences. Each of these versions presents Psyche as an emerging feminine soul, one who ultimately realizes against all odds that deep erotic love is the very ground of her being. The trials and travails required of Psyche to be joined with Eros deliver her to a personal sovereignty such as she had never experienced before in her life.

Each telling of the tale reveals how Psyche sets about to achieve the integration of her mortal self with her divine self. Psyche does not attempt this integration by *transcending* but rather by *experiencing deeply* the everyday realities of life. Through risk, vulnerability, and when necessary, panic and suffering, she *experiences* the profoundly healing truth that body and soul are one. Led by the nonhuman voices of the natural world, she unmasks the illusion of the separateness of body and soul, and doing so, she recovers the connections of her sacred earthliness and her earthly divinity. Scott offers:

> *To claim her divinely given right to know her self, her man, and the meaning of love, and to become who she could be and enjoy erotic love, Psyche had to disobey what she and Eros had been taught was right and good and true. She had to experience panic and bear the wrath of the culture that condemned her. In order to develop the self she had found and regain her erotic love, Psyche gambled and undertook four high-risk tasks. And so must every woman who wants to be happy.*

Myth is a kind of language largely misconstrued. It is neither precise nor pedantic. The language of myth is organic, juicy, and non-rational—kindled by the songs that rise from the strong body of the Earth through our bodies and our sensual thresholds. Like mist over a marshland, an enduring myth can take many shapes. Mythic language arises in our biology. It is the language that indicates and discloses our feelings, and our feelings change like the weather.

Ripe with meaning and highly resistant to being dammed up as dogma, mythic awareness concerns the way the world is, not necessarily the way the world should be. This awareness is ceaselessly pregnant with liminal and numinous possibilities. Myths move like rivers and currents of air through our lived lives. Myths love the human mind and have shaped the human mind. Unlike literalistic approaches and attitudes toward religious scriptures, myths never insist that one meaning fits all. Myths compose our first stories. They are the songs of our souls.

In *Myth and Meaning,* Claude Lévi-Strauss, the anthropologist not the jeans designer, posits that particular cultural codes can be cracked by discovering the myths that inform that culture—and what meanings those myths bequeath to individuals living within it. At the time the myth of Psyche and Eros sprang into my life, I was dog-paddling shoreward from the undertow of some disappearing dreams and disappointing times. My acting career was hardly to be seen, and existed mostly in reruns, resumes, and depleted residuals. With my writing career, I was struggling to be solvent. My marriage was fracturing into pieces I could not fix or sort out. And the ticking of my biological clock, seriously amplified by midlife hormones, was impossible to silence. A sense of failure stalked me, eroding my impossibly upbeat days, eventually eclipsing just about anything I'd ever been enthusiastic about or thought I'd accomplished. When friends, or on occasion even someone I was auditioning for, asked why I wasn't a star, I felt a little like Brando—"I coulda' been a contender." But somehow I had missed the boat. For whatever reasons, and they're plentiful for hopefuls like myself who never quite *made it,* starhood rode off into a less than memorable cinematic sunset.

Strange as it seems now, I was not an outwardly broken, muddled heap during the worst of those times. I excel in coping and minimizing, to a fault. I'm quite a little champ at what psychotherapist and author Harriet Lerner calls "over-functioning." It was a little like the line from the Steve Martin movie, *L.A. Story,* "I was depressed, but I didn't know it because I was so happy." This was rather true of me. I was not unduly depressed, except for moments, nor overwhelming unhappy, except for moments, but something shadowy my way came. Over time, the feelings packed into this period of my life felt like a loss of faith in myself, and in my life's purpose. Without realizing it, I had given up on living the dream dearest and deepest in my heart—which was to have a true and deeply erotic love, a love affair with life, one that lasts when one's eyes are wide open. I'm not sure when Eros first visited me, but I think it was probably with animals and my first encounters in the outdoors. My mother said my first words were not *Mommy* or *Daddy* but *Bow-wow*. Of course it may have been when Tommy Good (his actual name) sparked something in me when I was about eight years old!

When I arrived to take up my life quest in Hollywood, Eros flew in with a full quiver of arrows. Eros appeared in every nook and cranny of my life, in my career and its struggles, in my love affairs, in friendships, continuing in nature, in my marriages, and in surprising times thereafter. Each time Eros appeared in my life, I felt open not only to an expanded and deeply embodied sense of Self but also to a rushing windfall of creativity. Eros is an intrinsically sacred dynamic between men and women, or any romantic combination, between Heaven and Earth, between pretty much everything vibrating between the moon and New York City, or in my case, Hollywood. Of course, for a great many people, Hollywood is practically synonymous with Eros, being as it is the Mt. Olympus of fantasy life.

In truth, I really wasn't all that cogent about Eros back in the day. But I can see now how inextricably I was enlivened by it—ducking and plucking arrows through the adventures of every day, writing and singing songs of paradise one day and heartbreak the next. A dreamy-eyed lass was I, the prototypical woman for whom the great storyteller Clarisa Pinkola Estes wrote her classic book *Women Who Run with the Wolves*. I was running with the wolves, being as I love wolves and dogs, hampered by an idealism real wolves would find wanting. Eros cannot be tamed by idealism. Fortunately.

What do I mean by *erotic* love? Mary Hugh Scott's definition sits well enough with me:

> *The kind of emotion that pierces the human heart, causing people to care consciously and passionately about one another. The unexplainable magnetism that draws people together in mutual devotion. More especially it is the deep irrational affection that unites a man and woman in an*

enchanted relationship. The power of erotic love opposes death (unconsciousness) and overcomes it.

Longing for deeply felt erotic love doesn't seem particularly fashionable nowadays—or at least to admit to longing for it. We are expected to have wised up *by now*, had enough therapy *by now*, read enough self-help books about addictions to love, etc., to realize all that erotic stuff is infused with projections and immature romantic feelings, etc. In these postmodern times, erotic love doesn't hold up very well under the highly magnifying electron microscopes of analytical vivisection. Sensible love and rational love are rarely considered to be erotic love, and yet, erotic love seems to me eminently sensible and rational. The erotic has degenerated into perverse fragments of its original pulse. A very visible image of this is the potent, manly image of Eros that has now been reduced to the childish image of a rosy-cheeked Cupid with a pudgy bottom. Cupid is so young, a baby really. Adorable he may be, and certainly able to inspire immense feelings—but when was the last time you saw a baby seriously use a bow and gold-tipped arrow?

It sounds naive, simplistic, unsophisticated, even dangerous, to yearn for a sustainable, awakened, and deeply erotic love inflicted by a powerful force. Well-meaning and wise therapeutic and spiritual gurus may try to persuade us that the quest for erotic union primarily concerns the intimacy we need and want from God, and that once found, this god love affair alone should satisfy. In some cases, it just might, as we know from the thrillingly erotic poetry of Rumi. For myself, however, I wasn't sure that God was something all that different from some man I might fall in love with. I felt that falling in love with a person is to be falling in love with God. At least for me. I already loved God a lot, but the prevailing concepts of God left out one thing that I tend to cling to for dear life, my body, and a second thing, of course, the body of the Earth.

In the book *Anam Cara*, John O'Donohue writes:

> *The body has had such a low and negative profile in the world of spirituality because spirit has been understood more in terms of the air element than the earth element.... When you confine spirit to this region alone, the physical becomes diminished. This is a great mistake, for there is nothing in the Universe as sensuous as God.*

Psyche doesn't leave her body behind to search for some patriarchal, scriptural ideal of salvation and redemption. Her body, an integral aspect of her being allured by and filled with feelings of Eros, facilitates her journey of self-discovery.

Fortunately, not everyone is captive to the scenario that intense passion must be relinquished as we grow older. Harriett Lerner once spoke in L.A. at a forum sponsored by Actresses@Work, a group I was involved with, which was intent on changing perceptions of midlife women by promoting roles that reflect our lives more authentically. Lerner's theme was "The Greatest Stories Never Told," and as co-editor of our group's newsletter, I was there to record her remarks. Referring to women over fifty, she said "women often find the greatest love of their lives at this time; a truer, deeper passion."

When the myth of Psyche and Eros entered my life, it cut me open like a ripe melon. I was waiting for that cut, that vulnerable opening where nature would pierce me through with unerring wisdom about myself. My pilgrimages back and forth into this myth are the musings of a midlife woman entering thresholds of her maturing self, which before I discovered and read the myth I could barely perceive. As time went by, I was more and more able to meet my own story as it unfolded through the lens of this myth.

What I recognized was that once upon a mythological time another woman, Psyche, a mere mortal like me, living amongst many life-altering gods, goddesses, and events, had desires, thoughts, and concerns not unlike my own. In particular, her desire to regain her lost love, her Eros, moved through her with fierce longing. As Psyche would come to understand, Eros had something to do with a longing for personal sovereignty. I immediately caught the scent of that longing. Like Psyche, I too sought the merging of a divine beloved with a beloved possessing a human face. Like me, she wanted to know and see deeply the man she loved, all those people and things she loved, and love itself—and to be known and seen in return. And like Psyche, I was young—except in her case, her youthfulness was appropriate to her biological age.

With Psyche I came to understand what a perilous journey, filled with seemingly insurmountable tasks, must be undertaken to find (or regain) a relationship with Eros—to find a love which ribbons deep feeling through the clay landscape of our bodies, the visible landscape of the Earth, and the invisible landscape of our dreams. This is to seek after a love that celebrates flesh and spirit in oneness. This is a love that doesn't require a woman to give up any parts of herself, especially the divining rods of her senses, or her ability to enter into the complexities and paradoxes of life. This is a love that honors and values the wisdom of a woman alongside that of a man, the essential wisdom of the feminine and the masculine passionately entwined in equal measure, multi-voiced and unifying. This love endures the often spirit-killing jobs, deals, and deeds that are done to pay the rent, buy the groceries, cover the insurance premiums protecting every little thing that might go wrong, slip away, and/or break down. This love ignites the self towards its fullest capacity to experience earthly and divine pleasures. This is love on fire with life. Yes, it is a lot to ask for, and perhaps that's why we often give up before the journey even begins.

The journey that Psyche undertakes to be reunited with her beloved Eros can be characterized as the journey of individuation. This is the process of becoming autonomous, of bringing into existence one's individuality while eagerly engaging intimate relationship with others. Inherent in this process are the elemental ingredients each person must discover within herself or himself to engage life authentically, spontaneously, and joyfully. This also requires journeys into the shadow lands. There, in the unclaimed territories within us, in the shadows where we place parts of ourselves in exile and denial, a synthesizing maturity has opportunity to bloom.

Psyche's journey eventually involves four specific and titanic tasks, the kinds of challenges for which the gods and goddesses are famously known in their testing the mettle and sanity of us mere mortals. Like me, Psyche often feels she is not up for the next task required of her in her journey of individuation. Like me, Psyche almost gives up, but she never does. Like me, she finds help when she needs it most. Psyche, when I listen to her, that is, when I listen to my own soul, does not allow me to turn back. She and I seem to share some essential knowing that in the deepest natural self, a woman may yearn for the life that has been denied her for thousands of years. The memory of that life shimmers and stirs in haunting ways within many women, and within the men who love them.

Something else Psyche told me—and this I surely didn't want to hear—is that I must risk everything to find Eros, knowing I may never find the love I seek. *Trust,* I hear Psyche say. Trust that whether I find this love or not, the journey towards it will change my way of being in the world forever, and this change is worth every step of the journey. It will perhaps be a gift, a boon, to others as well. My regret, she hints, will be if I hold back, if I try to think my way through the journey ahead, weighing and fearing the possible losses and consequences. *You know what it is you want,* she kept saying to me. *Do you have the courage to go after it, knowing it may never be yours?*

I wasn't sure I did. I'm still not. But the journey has begun, and it is definitely changing me. Thus far it is worth every step and misstep, every doubt, every quaking emotion, and every tear. There are good days and bad days, and the days that feel eerily "comfortable" like the good ole days when I was clueless. But the seeds planted in my soul by this myth have been rhizogenic. Exuding the gumption of grass when it breaks through the sidewalks we've paved so we won't stumble on all those rooted things trying naturally to trip us up, the myth of Psyche and Eros continually breaks into my life—often when I least expect it.

I think the myth is especially life enhancing and empowering for women as we enter our middle years. It may take that long to rediscover and reclaim some voice, dream, truth, some something within us. Often it is something we once had but left behind, or something now appearing as if out of a forgetful fog. Only with sufficient "failures" and "accomplishments" are we prepared to appreciate the paradoxes and disappointments of life for the beneficial tensions they create in stretching us to fulfill ourselves. We have survived enough to know that *we can survive much*. In our older years we have become sufficiently discriminating to turn away from those people and circumstances that we may have allowed to carry us away from ourselves. Perhaps we even wanted to be carried away. But a time arrives for many of us when we begin to move towards unrealized longings. We yearn to balance, maybe even to override, the *reasonable* voices within preaching safety and certainty, asserting the voices of our intuition that are leading us to *leap*. When this moment does arrive for a woman, she may not always be championed from where she might like, or by whom she hopes will support her. But this I do know to be true—help sometimes arrives just when we need it most, often in the most unimaginable ways.

A woman who is confronting the prodigious tasks of her own individuation not only increases the likelihood of joy smelting her life, but she also deepens her own personal sense of sovereignty. Once wrested from the multi-voiced layers of life, sovereignty is, as Danny Kaye puts it in the movie *The Court Jester*, "the chalice from the palace . . . the brew which is true." The authentic feminine, the brew which is true, is the best of all possible brews for a man to drink heartily from, to enrich and deepen his own authentic masculine. Much unhappiness roams the Earth because men, still (by and large) the rulers of the world, are not given what they need to be *good* kings. They are often afraid to drink deep from the feminine brew that is true. Men need women and women need men in the fullness of our mutual capacities for erotic love in all its many forms.

Those who ransack the natural world and the cosmic fires inherent in our indigenous nature rob both men and women of the erotic sweetness we thrive on to be fully human. The bad kings, patriarchs, and tyrants of religious and social dogmas tell us our bodies and our sensations mislead us, that these are not good or decent feelings and certainly not divine, and not ever to be honored by being pleasured. Better to mummify them under plastic slipcovers so life can't ooze through the body's exquisitely permeable skin with sticky liquids and uncontrollable feelings. We, the great sperm swimmers of the water planet, are told that we are not to enjoy our moistness, our wetness, emotionally, or physically—and so forth, and so forth. And in the sway of the sad and bad kings, few men are truly capable of relishing and enjoying their desire to penetrate women deeply—nor are women able to relish being penetrated. Thus we experience a planet of unravished lovers, struggling to hold on to Eros as best we can.

Erotic love is the human manifest of the drive of this deeply alive planet forever dancing chaos into harmonies, dissonances, yearnings, pleasures, and the fullness of life that Eros brings forth. Only when the rulers of this world, the rulers that exist in each of us, can without guilt value the feminine as much as they value the masculine will the extreme violence affecting every part of our lives begin to dissipate. When men and women are free to pursue and embody flexible, non-dogmatic worldviews, the wholeness, goodness, and all-rightness of erotic love could usher in a new reality for our kind.

The myth of Psyche and Eros arose in the world of ancient Greece—not exactly my world, though much that is Greek clearly continues to influence and shape contemporary thought. This is the nature of the archetypes. It is easy for me to see in Psyche attributes of myself, at least as I remember myself as a younger woman. I then inhabited a richly numinous world, physically, sensually, emotionally, and especially in nature. It was not unusual for me as a young child to strip off my clothes, plaster my naked body with wet leaves from a stream, and dance like Dionysus across the lawn into the woods. Growing into a young woman, I continuously experienced and exuded a very centering sort of love for wild places and animals, and for untamed people. A tree could inspire as much a sense of the numinous as a church, and this becomes even more so as I grow older.

Like Psyche, as a younger woman, I also had a range of mundane expectations to be met, pedestals to ascend, perfections to emulate and embody. Sometimes boys, and later men, found me unapproachable, or perhaps not easily approachable, since I had this otherworldly sheen about me coexisting with an acute shyness that overtook me in my teen years. Only in the last few years have I come to realize how much of that sheen might have been a sort of protection against the grittier realities of life. Also, like Psyche, I had parents whom I loved and for whom I would have done most anything with the same kind of innocent bravery with which Psyche faces the mountain when her parents deposit her there. Like Psyche, I saw my parents' needs as being my own. Such feelings stayed with me long into adulthood.

Psyche may have clung to her own sense of goodness, or if you will, all-right-ness, also as protection. Had I been facing the cold, dark, mountain of an uncertain and possibly terrifying future, I might have fed myself Disney-like fantasies of being rescued by someone who would recognize my goodness. My sense of my own goodness seemed to me to be my salvation against harm and terrors, nameless or otherwise. *If only I can be good enough, I will be safe*—was my unconscious mantra. As a youth and far into my adult years, I had stalwart trust that when bad things befell me I would be delivered by a loving God. Early in my childhood, I experienced a deliverance from a powerfully life-shaping set of circumstances. Several years after my parents' devastating divorce that placed my brother and me in an orphanage, my mother came to retrieve us. A similar deliverance happens to Psyche. Rather than succumbing to the dark god Thanatos, Psyche is rescued by none other than the God of Love himself, Eros, sent by his wrathful mother Aphrodite.

On that mountain, high above the world that had been her young life, Psyche waits, as women often wait, for her future to arrive. The malicious threads that Aphrodite weaves ultimately become the golden threads of Psyche's transformation. Thus we encounter the delectable irony at the heart of this story. In the *human* Psyche's daring encounter with *goddess* Aphrodite, the human emerges victorious. Psyche's natural grace and courage to follow where her deepest longing leads, offer possibilities for healing the split between the mortal and divine—for women and for men.

And so our story takes a turn other than the one Aphrodite has plotted. Rather than condemning Psyche to death, Aphrodite's son helps Psyche embody a story for all women who cannot or choose not to follow the prescriptions and paradigms that prevail. These women carry the creed of the heroine's quest as the healing heart within the dreams and desires of our lives.

Although this story unravels through Psyche's perspective, her journey propels both her and Eros into deepening maturity. Each helps the other even when they are apart and have no assurances that they will ever find each other again.

The location where Psyche and Eros meet is telling. It is where most lovers meet—on a mountaintop, in the dark. Which is to say, they meet in a place of high emotional excitement and possibility, where the view is breathtaking, whenever one might chance to see it beyond gazing upon the beloved. Psyche and Eros, our lovers, meet outdoors, not inside some protected space, for they are beyond themselves—beyond the separating of selves armored against unsettling and all-consuming feeling. Like all lovers, Psyche and Eros become permeable by the transforming spirit of their passion. They move into each other, melting barriers between themselves and the physical world. They can do this even though they are strangers to each other and still very much in the dark, maybe *even because* they are strangers and in the dark. The fertile night caresses them like warm loam around freshly planted seeds. It is a delicious darkness from whence their love will grow. No wonder we say that we are *falling* in love with someone. It is an awesome letting go, this falling, and in Psyche's case, falling down into the dark is at the heart of all she comes to discover.

Nothing un-tethers one from dogma and patriarchal abstractions of *should* and *shouldn't* like Eros. Eros delivers lovers into the very sap of life. When Psyche and Eros make love, Psyche experiences a radiance never felt before. She embodies the ancient yearnings within a woman, young or old, for those exalted moments that are sparked and quickened by the masculine touch. When dawn licks at the edges of this heavenly night, Eros, convinced he has found the woman he wishes for himself, implores his sidekick Zephyrus, the West Wind, to bring Psyche to his extraordinary ranch in the green hills of Montana, except in those days it was Greece. A devoted friend and wind for all reasons and seasons, Zephyrus is glad to be an accomplice to the lovers and carries out the command of Eros with tenderness and breezy panache. Before the sun spills into the valley below, Zephyrus plucks the ravished Psyche from the mountaintop and gently lays her upon the still sleeping violets in the tree-encircled meadow below.

Awakening from her night of lovemaking, Psyche is unsure where she is. She is, of course, in the lush green meadow that grows instantly between two lovers when the erotic pulse has touched them deeply. This is the field of all possibilities. She is deliciously disoriented, altered. Masculine penetration ripples through her as she looks about and sees life in a way she has never quite seen it before—bursting with dew and flowers opening their hearts to the warming sun, as she has opened hers.

As dawn brightens, an utterly magnificent residence, just visible in a nearby grove of trees, allures Psyche. Still unsure what has befallen her, and not a little apprehensive that Thanatos may yet pounce upon her, she passes through the grove and cautiously approaches the palace. Up close the estate is overwhelming, a veritable candidate for the pages of *Architectural Digest*. Psyche has never seen such a house. It is a dwelling fit for a god, which, of course, it is. The desire to enter overpowers her, and so she does, but not without trepidation. Once inside, much to her amazement, barely audible, musical voices beckon her. These are the voices of intuition and the voices of living things that inform intuition. From this moment on, these voices grow stronger, prompting Psyche continually to explore and engage the riches of the physical world and not be afraid of what seems strange. The wealth she encounters in this house will prove to be far more than the masonry, gold, and jewels that compose it. It is a sacred house that will eventually become a golden prison and the impetus for Psyche to follow her heart and intuition as never before.

The fairy-like voices heard by Psyche in these sumptuous corridors lead her through rooms of unsurpassed splendor and abundance. Rubies, sapphires, and emeralds glitter from walls of gold. Marble floors shine like arctic ice floes. Precious silk tapestries hang as if alive upon the walls high above exquisitely woven rugs of the most expensive fabrics that soften her every footfall. As satin drapes flutter from tall, arching windows, the day's amber light spills upon luxuriously enticing furniture. The beauty of these surroundings enthralls her.

As she steps into the dining room, a magnificent feast steaming forth its savories, draws Psyche to sit and eat. While eating, she again hears that manly voice that has so potently stirred her senses, as Eros declares his love and intentions. If Psyche will obey his command never to see him in the light of day and never to ask him questions about his whereabouts when he leaves, she will nightly experience their ecstatic coupling, his devoted protection, and all the riches the house contains and more will be hers.

Well, who of us wouldn't be swept away? A resounding *Yes!* courses through Psyche. The promise she must make to inhabit this paradise opening up before her seems insignificant in the golden light of her love for Eros. Most women, certainly I, can identify with these little *concessions* we may make at the beginning of a love affair or a marriage. They appear to be niggling things barely perceived in the penumbral light of new love. We accept such concessions without fanfare because we rarely consider their implications. We may wonder, but usually we don't: Is not our beloved also accepting of what *teensy imperfections* we may possess? In our naive grasp of what we imagine paradise to be, many women like me often and inadvertently sacrifice a certain maturity to uphold a childlike and innocent version of paradise, and thus, perhaps, preserve an attachment to our own young maidenhood.

Some myths and fairytales, as well as Jungian perspectives, suggest that marriage is a kind of death for women but not so for men. In the patriarchal scheme of things, a woman's world is altered far more dramatically by marriage than is a man's. While her stature and status tend to diminish, his tend to increase. Of course, not all women and couples are in bondage to the changes marriage often imposes. Even so, when a woman chooses fervently to embrace marital changes, she may, as time goes by, feel an encroaching ambivalence, that she has left parts of her self behind in order to nurture and sustain the dreams of another, or others. When the voice of Eros turns a woman's world upside down with a promise of paradise, it can be irresistible.

When I first read this myth, I embraced marriage with open arms, far more excited and enlivened by what I imagined I was moving towards rather than wary about what I might be leaving behind. Working through the myth and the many interpretations, I pulled back a few veils.

Remembering the little girl I had been, a Dionysian dancer leaping across any available lawns, I came to realize that sometime between this leafy youthfulness and the period during which I took on the exactitudes of patriarchal perfection, I had said goodbye to parts of myself. In fact, by the time I got married, I had fairly well chosen perfectionism and idealism over authenticity. I didn't know I had chosen this, not consciously anyway, but to a good extent, I had indeed split off aspects of myself.

In *Psyche and Eros, Mind and Gender in the Life Course*, Gisela Labouvie-Vief offers tremendous insights with regard to this process of forsaking parts of ourselves as we grow up—as is prevalent among females and males. Labouvie-Vief observes:

> *In the process of mastering the rules of our culture, we learn to be good sons and daughters of our culture, to idealize ourselves along the guidelines provided by that culture. The advantage we gain from this process of self-idealization is that we are able to participate in the riches our culture has to offer: protection, security, knowledge, so on. But we also pay a price for these cultural gifts. To become a good member of the collective, the individual must renounce more spontaneous and instinctual forms of behavior.*

To understand better this tendency to forsake parts of who we are, it is helpful to ask, who is it that tells Psyche's father that she must be brought to the mountain to appease Aphrodite's discontent? It is the Oracle who serves Apollo. Apollo, of course, is the twin brother of Dionysus. In earlier times, though highly different personalities, the natures of these twin brothers were considered complementary. However, over time their complementary natures are lost and eventually they are pitted in dramatic opposition to one another. Dionysus is eclipsed by Apollo as a new and emerging consciousness takes hold.

Apollo becomes the template of perfectionism. His behavior exalts the rational as the main avenue to wisdom. He is the sun and the light of a new day. He is, in fact, the Golden Mean to everything the modern world comes to cherish—perfect measurements, crisp boundaries, scientific certainties, and predictable outcomes. In other words, he is the model for heroic, rational perfectionism. As Apollo's star rises in the imagination of the Western mind, Dionysus falls into dishonor and disgrace, taking with him his ecstatic, intoxicating, unpredictable, and irrational dancing into the heart of wisdom. In short, Dionysus can't keep down a job. Ironically, it is Dionysus who loves and appreciates the sensuality of women. A lot! Dionysus moves in women's dreams with his sensual darkness and outlaw seductions, and remains here, for the most part even today, only a few heartbeats away from a woman's wildest fantasies.

The split off parts of the self that are associated with Dionysus and the feminine constellate in the shadows of Eurocentric culture. Through the millennia, women have become the carriers of these undervalued, shadowed aspects of our organic, animistic, instinctual, emotional, intuitional, and non-rational selves. Quite a lot to leave behind, if you think about it—and, of course, *let's!*

Both women and men have been under the spell of Apollo's Creed, as I call it, and its principles of rationality, but it is women who usually feel the split off and forsaken parts of themselves most acutely. We may honor the Apollonian path that we in the West chose to achieve certain awareness and fulfillment, but Apollo is only one of two brothers. Bereft of the influence of Dionysus, the domineering Apollo has produced a world of horrifying and crippling imbalances. This could be why native cultures are so appealing to those of us from religious backgrounds that split apart sacredness and earthiness. Split off from the wholeness of our nature, we turn to *stuff* and substances to dull the heartache and the homesickness left by the missing elements of our nature. We are no longer at home in the place that gave birth to us—the Earth. Without Gaia and her chaos, Eros is homeless. As a result, many of us yearn to dance again with our friend Dionysus, with our lovers, our men friends, and our women friends. We long to feel the dance and the mystery of life romancing our bones.

Thus it is that Psyche and Eros marry and enter the honeyed kingdom of the honeymoon, the Paradise moments of their love, when they are enlivened by mystery and romance. I know this kingdom. With many newlyweds, in the beginning, the intense attraction between Psyche and

Eros illuminates our very private, intimate world with a precious and rosy, otherworldly light. Every night Eros comes to Psyche, whispers her name, clasps her tenderly, and sends his ardor through every pore of her being. Their combined rapture softens even the hardest edges of daily life.

For a period of time, Psyche delights in her love, her good fortune, her very own home, and she relishes her hearth-keeping, her homemaking, her Hestian queendom. Transforming dust into gleaming surfaces, rearranging furniture, cooking healthy and gourmet meals, surprising Eros with a good bottle of wine, divining the optimum locations for reading and sacred lamps—in short, making a sanctuary for herself and her man Eros—floods Psyche with wellbeing.

Hallelujah! I heartily identify with Psyche's domestic happiness, filling vases with wildflowers and bowls with fruit, arranging and rearranging the photos, the collected seashells and rocks, dishing up vegetables from the garden. When Eros comes through that door, or in his case perhaps, winging through a window, at the end of the day, he enters a home that replenishes whatever the workaday world has taken from him. After all, being the god of Love has got to be taxing at times.

Through huge chunks of time, this outlook has been enough for me. I am a woman who deeply loves home, perhaps because of the gypsy-like situation in my younger life. Though it is not the only way I feel fulfilled, I receive much satisfaction breathing spirit into a house and making it home. I enjoy creating and offering a living space to my man, my Eros, as an expression of who I am. But had my life been a replica of Psyche's, eventually I would grow tired of never exploring the world outside my safe and familiar surroundings, and I would miss the laughs and good times one shares with friends. As rapturous as my meetings and lovemaking with Eros might be, never to behold his beloved face would be unbearable. Not sharing the worlds he visits within and without would cause me to grow sad. In time, I too, would feel distress over his undisclosed life away from me. And, in time, I too, would chaff under his need to control our life to suit his purposes and his secrets. Enough of these patterns have played through my life to allow me to empathize with Psyche's journey.

It is no doubt true, as Robert Johnson puts it in *She: Understanding Feminine Psychology,* that "all paradises fail. Each one has a serpent in it that demands the opposite of the peace and tranquility of the Garden of Eden." In Western mythologies, the Garden of Eden and the serpent are archetypal images of what goes wrong in the world, or in a relationship. The serpent is indeed a most potent icon of the Goddess. When the ancient Goddess cultures were eclipsed, the snake, a once highly venerated symbol of the feminine force of nature, nurturance, power, and wisdom, became reviled. In patriarchal parlance, when things go wrong, blame it on the snake, and kill it.

It was Eve who did something unforgivable by listening to the serpent. What a diabolical wench! We've been led to believe that if it weren't for Eve's disobedience, we might still be blithely trooping around in skimpy leisurewear without a care in the world. However, on the other hand, Eve's response, sharing with Adam that apple they were forbidden to experience and savor, has forever after kept the serpentine conversation of consciousness going. Something, I think, we should be grateful for. To this day, we little understand the link between consciousness and eros. The myth of Psyche and Eros, in fact, suggests that the initial intensity of erotic love often doesn't last because it is not sufficiently *conscious* of all that Eros involves, including the vexing matters of dissolving boundaries and the destabilizing of our established senses of self. As much as we want to fall in love, who really wants to be *that* vulnerable?

It is no easy thing to sustain erotic love in a patriarchal world that aims to dominate the unpredictable and emasculate the mysterious. It is the rare couple for whom Eros catches fire for life. Most erotic love withers. Yet, deep desire is the momentous gift that Psyche offers to all of us—that is, the commitment to life's erotic possibilities. Psyche ultimately *disobeys* those troubling voices that would prevent her from experiencing Eros in the light of day and in the light of her own knowing. By undertaking some formidable tasks to know herself unencumbered by the proscriptions and expectations of society, including those of pushy gods and goddesses, Psyche bequeaths the story that might just set us free to find the kind of love she was looking for and found, and to cultivate what may keep Eros alive.

In the early sparkle of an erotic relationship there is the oceanic feeling which only love bestows, that all is right with the world. Bumps in the road, say a flat tire on the way to the picnic, are barely felt, and when they are, they seem effortlessly overcome. But even as the sweetness of her love for Eros increases, Psyche becomes lonely and sad as the weeks and months roll by. She longs to see the face of the man who moves her to her depths and whose seed has begun to grow new life within her. And so, when Psyche hears that her sisters, believing she is dead, are deeply grieving, she implores Eros to let them visit.

The sisters, we soon realize, are wildly jealous of Psyche's good fortune. Their marriages, though conspicuous in status and wealth, are no match for the grandeur of Psyche's circumstances. That fact, however, is not what drives them to destroy Psyche. They see in her the luminosity of one permeated by divinely sensuous love. This is not the marriage either of them have. One is an Eternal Daughter, married to the older man whom she invests with all the qualities she wished for in a father. The other is the Eternal Mother-Caretaker, married to a crippled man. In Mary Hugh Scott's telling, both sisters are "unravished brides." Both are in relationships that kill passion and thwart true growth and transformation.

Though her sisters act as if they are well meaning, caring, and concerned for Psyche and her child—telling her that she is wed to a monster—they are in truth jealous of Psyche's life with Eros. When Psyche risks all those things women have been told they must have to be safe and to be loved, she may inadvertently challenge others to question their own life-choices. Such individuals may feel threatened by Psyche when she invites the dangers of the unknown rather than capitulating to a caged life, golden as it may be, of approval, supposed safety, and certainty. Bear in mind, the sisters also represent those chattering, doubting, castigating voices inside a woman, inner voices that sabotage the journey towards full selfhood. They want to control outcomes, want us to play by the rules.

The sisters devise a plan that exquisitely plays into the doubts and longings that are troubling Psyche. They freight Psyche's doubting voices with a gruesome scenario. They allege that there is something terribly wrong with Eros, that he is not who he makes himself out to be. Why can he only be with her in the dark? Why must he always vanish before the sun comes up? The sisters insinuate there is something wrong with Psyche herself to desire such an immature, unrealistic, and voracious love.

Dripping with false kindness, the sisters tell Psyche that the being who comes to her every night is a monstrous winged serpent, an ally of the oracle who dictated that she be abducted to the mountaintop. The people of the valley have seen this hideous creature, and it is known that he intends to kill her and the baby she is carrying. Psyche is loath to believe this. It cannot be. Not her Eros! Yet, the secretiveness, the refusal to be seen in the light, and certainly his having wings, fills her with uncertainty. Through a little crack of doubt, the evil sisters plant their treachery.

They have a great plan, they tell her. It will resolve all her doubts, and she will know for sure what she is dealing with. She is to have at the ready an oil lamp and a sharpened knife. After she and Eros have made love and he is sleeping, she is to light the lamp, bring it close to his face, and when she sees him for the monster that he is, she can whack off his head, save herself and her child. *Voilà!* Her problem will be solved.

But Psyche is greatly agitated, indeed, torn apart. She cannot bear to think of Eros as anything but the kindest, gentlest, most ardent man she has ever met. She has built a life predicated on this belief—as did I, and so many women. And yet, Psyche has given up things that once mattered to her in order to lie in the arms of Eros where she has felt the most sublime feelings she has ever known. Something has changed within her. With great courage and daring, holding all the contradictions of her predicament, including all the voices of doubt, Psyche decides to do the unthinkable. She chooses to gaze upon her beloved Eros in the light.

This may be the moment of greatest courage for a woman. She moves towards her beloved and towards her self, flush with her fears and anxieties, risking loneliness and reprisals, but willing to risk everything to bring what is in the dark between them into the light. This is the moment when a woman begins the descent into the fullness of herself, to visit those archetypal realms that have not yet been available to her. No longer slumbering in neglect, these aspects of her true self, now enlivened, bestow upon a woman the autonomy she craves and needs to be free and authentic. This self-assurance allows a woman to open herself vulnerably and instills in her the trust that no matter where love takes her, she will not *lose* herself in love but will *find* herself—over and over again.

When recognized and transformed, the voices of the malicious sisters can help us not to settle for deals and promises which steal away our spiritual radiance and feelings of erotic well-being. Paradoxically, Psyche's sisters propel her towards the tasks that she will encounter as she becomes a more fully conscious and mature woman. If we are successful at freeing ourselves from acceptable attitudes, we may, like Psyche, become more able to sustain the complexities of authentic love. A woman no longer willing to obey the edicts of the status quo can be a formidable individual.

That night as she waited for Eros to appear, Psyche was surely tormented by various options. She might have considered waiting for the winds of circumstance to change or for Eros to see how harmful the situation was to cultivating genuine intimacy. Perhaps, being a little too sympathetic about his difficult childhood, she could have continued to make excuses for his behavior. Of course, she might have thought the problem was primarily with her. After all, in so many ways they had a great life. Why not be content?

Women can be immensely talented at entertaining inventories like these. I was. But our gal Psyche was swifter to be bold than I might have been in her circumstance. She was no longer content to wait, as I was in certain aspects of my life. She was ready to risk everything, not even knowing what that might be. For the first time in her life, she took it upon herself to make a decision that was not in keeping with what was expected. In a dramatic departure from trying to be reasonable, she knows intuitively she cannot continue the way things are.

It isn't that Eros doesn't mean everything to her. *Au contraire*—he has meant everything, and he means more now that Psyche is *more* than a maiden. She has changed. As good as things are, something is missing. As she is beginning to embrace the risks and allow the mistakes of being a mature woman, she feels forces prompting her to seek with greater clarity what it is that burns so brightly between herself and her lover. She wants to *know* this man who wings about like a god, insisting only to be present to *her* in the dark. Indeed, without light between them, how can *he* know *her* as she really is?

Thus, a two-edged sword: Life with Eros is great but always on his terms. If I insist on some terms of my own, I may risk our intimacy—and risk appearing to be less than an unconditionally loving and supportive woman. After all, is that not my primary identity? Psyche is a mortal woman, and she wants to know Eros as a mortal man who is not, in every instance, acting godlike. It can be hurtful at times, living out this fantasy of his youthful mind, while he remains little acquainted with what she most truly values about herself. While Psyche still rides on the wings of her youthful fantasies, she also feels pulled towards a more complete union that will join her lover's divine powers with her unique and mortal self in the intimacies of a whole relationship. In *The Goddess,* Christine Downing notes of Hera, *she wants to be fully met.* This is the relationship to Eros that Psyche wants in her marriage. To know if this is a real possibility—and possibly it isn't—she must see her beloved in the light of day.

Psyche's intuition blazes, a fire she dare not put out. She may never have trusted or needed to trust her intuition quite to this extent. Which is to say again, Psyche doesn't know logically what it is that she is doing. And that's the wonder of it—that she can love this much, and risk what she loves, for something she can barely grasp. Tidy little *thoughts* don't line up on perfect perches to instruct her. Her intuitive *feelings* speak loud and clear throughout her entire body. Psyche is living differently now, dangerously, without a net, without a map. Though she cannot yet know it, her life will never be the same. So it was with me. As I stopped trying to think my way through the puzzlements in my life and relied more on my feelings to guide me, my life became more unstuck.

As the sun lengthens its shadows across the valley and the stars began ever so faintly to fill the sky, Psyche fills her lamp with oil and sharpens her knife. These are two perfect symbols: The lamp of the gentle feminine lights the darkness with moonlike fingers. The knife of the fierce feminine pares away falsehood of any kind. It never settles for laws and rules that deny the realness of the Earth and the body. A saying of Jesus, in a message of love, refers to the bringing of a sword. It is a powerful symbol, the deadly weapon as well as the scalpel of healing surgery. We do well, as Jung suggests, to consider Nietzsche's injunction, "Discern or perish!"

How Psyche must have trembled waiting for Eros to arrive. What might she have felt when she entered his arms that night and felt the pounding heat of his body press into hers, knowing she had plotted an act which could destroy the most cherished aspect of her life, her love for Eros? How close might she have come to losing her resolve, hoping against hope that something else might happen sparing her this act? What miracle might allow her to view this god-man whose animal and spiritual sweetness rivered through her long after he had flown away, without having to do her terrible deed?

As Eros sleeps, Psyche softly steals from their bed to the knife waiting by the unlit lamp. She lights the lamp and grasps the knife. Quaking but committed, she approaches the bed and brings the lamp close to the soft, warm covers she has just slipped out from under. She gasps. Lying before her is Love himself. Psyche is transformed by what she sees and what she feels. In an instant, her invisible fantasy lover becomes visible. This releases Psyche from being captive to a love that holds her in the dark. This moment transforms her into a woman who shines a lamp on love so she may awaken her lover and herself to Love's most conscious light. As Psyche gazes upon Eros, she notices his quiver of arrows. She takes one out to admire its delicate beauty. She accidentally pricks her finger and thus seals her love with Love.

In Erich Neumann's words:

> *She is no longer a victim, but an actively loving woman. She is in love, enraptured by Eros, who has seized her as a power from within, no longer as a man from with out....This knowing Psyche, who sees Eros in the full light, has broken the taboo of his invisibility, is no longer naive and infantile in her attitude toward the masculine; no longer merely captivating and captivated.*

It is this transformed Psyche who bends close to her lover's face to shower it wantonly with kisses, but as she does, she spills a drop of oil on his shoulder, and he awakens with a start. As might be expected from a god who designs his intimate encounters in the dark, when Eros sees his beloved Psyche standing there, lamp in one hand, knife in the other, his face contorts with an expression for which there is no term even in ancient Greek. And whose wouldn't? Let's give the god a break. With rage and reproach, and without giving Psyche a chance to say a word, he snaps up his toga and his quiver and bolts toward the window. Instantly realizing that he is no longer in control of things, he only desires to escape. He opens his strong wings and flies forth, just as Psyche grabs his right leg. Up, up, and away! She clings to him with all her might. Finally, she cannot hold on any longer and falls back to Earth. As he flies out of sight, she hears his parting words, "The child you carry will not be a god. It will be mortal."

Let's talk for a moment about our boy Eros, forever the boy, who, as we know, when things are no longer going his way flies back to Mama Aphrodite and her house and world. We will not see Eros again until the last act. What happens to him while he is away we can only surmise, but he goes through some upheavals on his own after he *drops* Psyche and vanishes in a huff. However it comes about, his change of heart will prove pivotal to his reunion with Psyche.

What we do know about Eros at this point of time in our tale is he can only be with a woman as a divinity, and while he offers a life of sublime goddess-hood to Psyche, that is not what she aspires to. Being worshipped and adored as a goddess is the flip side of being scorned and undervalued like a prostitute. Many a woman will accept a pedestal, not able to see the trap it sets for her if she desires to be a fully conscious woman, erotically alive with passion and personal sovereignty.

In his book, *Lying With the Heavenly Woman: Understanding and Integrating the Feminine Archetypes in Men's Lives,* Robert Johnson argues that the biggest challenge facing a man who strives to realize his own maturity is dealing with his mother complex: "The mother complex is his wish to regress to infancy again and to be taken care of, to crawl into bed and pull the covers over his head, to evade some responsibility that faces him. It can come as a mood, as a discouragement, as a paralysis, or as just being 'fed up' with it all."

It is important for a man to realize that his mother complex does not simply derive from his relationship with his actual mother or mother figure. Though sometimes a mother's relationship with her son intensifies this challenge in a negative way, a man must attend to the mother complex even under the most favorable circumstances. Often a son is confused by his mother complex, whether amicable or unfavorable, when acting out various projections upon his own flesh and blood mother and/or his wife or other women. Truly extraordinary efforts are required for a man to recognize how the enormous powers of the mother complex affect his relationships with all women.

Eros is obviously a prime candidate for concern in this area. Although Aphrodite holds the reins on her son very tightly, she does so for exactly the same reasons that she puts Psyche through hell. Aphrodite champions red, wild, roaring life, the deepest, undiluted currents of feelings. When we fall prey to controls and commandments created by those who are afraid of the tensions and tides in our bodies and in the natural world, Aphrodite may jar us back to our senses inevitably and tumultuously. Consider the alcoholism, rampant addictions, and covert perversions that creep out from under sexually repressive and misogynist dogmas of religious institutions. Ditto for those family-and-hearth, flag-waving politicians whose sexual ventures lay suppressed until someone alerts the media that Senator So-and-so has a mistress—his true love, in fact—in Bolivia.

In the most basic terms of the mother complex, a man faces first of all the dilemma of distinguishing the love of his mother from that of his partner. He is challenged to cut the cord of regression that continually confirms his status as the obedient son. He must discern how patriarchy—equally harmful to both genders—kills his erotic spirit by separating the experience of his body from its animating sources. In our story, until Eros can feel his erotic allure with the woman he loves, he cannot be a fully initiated male who cherishes his own sexuality as much as anything in his life. Such a man cannot inhabit his life in its natural fullness. He will feel compelled to sublimate. He can be a poster boy for the written word, for various ideas elevating disembodied spirituality and so called righteousness, but if he gets no further than that, he will probably feel something glorious eluded him when it is time to say goodbye to life.

Until that moment when a man sufficiently frees himself from the entanglements of his mother complex, the options he perceives may be those of extremes. He might be the family-oriented, spiritually correct son, or the Hollywood version of the super-stud, or the lone cowboy riding into the sunset. However, the immense and deeply erotic green valley that he could find alongside his Beloved quite likely will remain beyond his reach.

Meanwhile, back at the myth, after the frenzied exit of Eros from her life, Psyche is more alone than she has ever been. She now has a taste of what deep love feels like. She has memories of a home where birdsong, beautiful windswept trees and gardens greeted her senses every morning. That love is now gone. She is bereft of what can give her a sense of belonging and being at home. No longer is she the maiden who can return to her parents for shelter. Well, she might, but she too would regress if she headed back home for too long a period of time. That would be a short-lived antidote to her loneliness at best. But neither is she yet the woman she is struggling to be. That woman remains barely perceptible to her.

Tanya Wilkinson, author of *Medea's Folly*, brings forward powerful insights about the double bind a woman often finds herself in:

> *Women and the feminine are all obstacles to the Western project of the transcendence of nature. At the same time women and the feminine are a refuge from the alienation, loss of meaning, and disenchantment, which transcending nature produces. This is a double bind for women, a situation in which they can neither feel good about being associated with nature nor can they feel good about trying to transcend nature.... How can she transcend the world while being responsible for making a cozy refuge in the world, for herself and her loved ones?*

When Eros flies away, Psyche's world collapses. The magnificent house vanishes, and with it the daily and meaningful—as is so for some women—duties of hearth keeping. The break-up of an erotic relationship is surely a tumultuous moment for a woman (as also for a man). Psyche cannot go back, yet she cannot see clearly any road to travel on. She enters despair with no easy formulas for an exit. Perhaps for the first time, Psyche realizes that those old concepts of *goodness* were not the unfailing allies she thought them to be. As her journey continues in ways mysterious and life-changing, other allies—not limited to her innocent sense of goodness—will arrive to provide inner and outer support, and to assist with the ripening of her personal empowerment.

The lofty mantle of girlhood and idealized womanhood are slowly falling away. Raw in her nakedness and vulnerability, Psyche longs for the absent Eros. She loves him all the more now because she has seen him. She cries herself to sleep. She fantasizes his coming to her when at last he realizes what she is to him. She makes love to him in her dreams. An all-consuming yearning arises, such that she has never known before. How poignant and delicate Eros looked as he breathed in his sleep. Finally she has seen what she hardly knew she was after. She has seen the man and even the animal in the god. His physical beauty stirs her, yes, but the vulnerability she detects even in his godhood is what truly draws her close to him. Underneath all the sound of wings and bravura she glimpses someone who, like herself, is quite undone by this stunning turn of events, a man who cannot handle everything as coolly as gods are supposed to.

And this is just as important: She has seen how quickly Eros flew away, without the slightest attempt at hearing her side of the story. In ways she will later come to understand, she has observed the shadow-side of Eros. Psyche begins to sense how the overwhelming intensity of this divine connection could consume and possibly destroy her, and how she must be attentive to the drive of Eros to control her. Psyche does not fall captive to cozy and seductive images of Eros that could blind her to the ensnaring horrors he might incite and inflict. That allure could turn into a compulsive fire of addiction, separating lovers from the rest of the world rather than uniting them with the deepest mysteries of life and themselves.

What Psyche needs at this time is to activate her intuition to engage the archetype of the animus—another Jungian notion. The animus is the inner masculine nature of a woman. It is doubtful Psyche was aware of her animus energies any more than I was! In my early sojourn in Hollywood, I was greatly drawn to the company of men. Having grown up mostly without my father, and with little of a strong masculine presence in my life, my first twenty years were shaped by a strong mother-daughter relationship. Looking back, it seems to me that girlfriends and boyfriends who needed mothering were often drawn to me—a function I took up at a young age. "If you can be a mother to your brother," my mother once said to me, "we can all live together" and thus, he and I would not have to go back to the orphanage. I took up her statement as a necessary challenge for keeping our little family together. Much later, my entrance into Hollywood brought me into a man's world as I had never been before. Erotic and romantic attraction beckoned to be sure, but I also gained a fuzzy sense that my career hinged at times on being more in touch with masculine attitudes—being more assertive and business-like, being able to "think like a man."

A few years ago, I attended the wedding of a young woman client of my husband. Something about the situation of this bride unnerved me. I felt envious in a way I didn't immediately understand. What was bothering me came to light when the father of the bride approached my husband and me with rave reviews about his daughter. "She's a smart cookie, that one," he said. "She knows how to take care of herself in the world. She knows never to take the first offer. She knows how to negotiate. She knows how to make a deal."

Well, there it was. I not only took the first offer but also often worked for no money at all. I thought I was doing the right thing, the *good* thing. Yes, this woman was a father-daughter, not a mother-daughter like myself. She knew things, practical, pragmatic things about being in the world. She had easy, playful, seductive, and even manipulating encounters with the opposite sex. It took me a long time to figure all this out.

Eventually I picked up on a few things, including how some masculine *differentiation* was important to my maturity, and for advancing my career. Like Psyche I sensed slumbering parts of myself waiting to be roused. Neither she nor I started out with a clear picture of what that entails, but here is where intuition takes center-stage. When intuition has a chance, it will reveal things as one meanders along, stumbling into discoveries. Intuition has served me well in life, and yet, how often I still muffle its voice. It may seem ironic, but Jung felt that women who embrace and develop their masculine attributes can become more individuated and happier and recognize more options for reckoning with life's challenges. The corollary is true for men when they develop their anima, their feminine nature. This brings to mind the movie, *Tootsie*, when Dustin Hoffman's character remarks, "I was a better man when I was a woman."

Until a woman is ready to explore and engage her many facets, even those she considers flawed and unworthy of love, she will never feel completely at home in her body, in the heart of her nature, or in the body of the world. It is a great gift to find a home within oneself and then to find a beloved who has also found a home within himself.

In folktales and myths, and ah, yes, in life itself, the journey within and without is not a linear one. Life is not a grid of straight lines. Life is a river that re-arranges itself daily. When she lets go of clinging to Eros, Psyche does not fall back to Earth, have a week or two of tearing her hair out and weeping, and then go, "Aha, now I see." She still doesn't grasp a whole lot. Yet, like me, she is on her way.

To be sure, Psyche is deeply heartbroken. No therapist can rub away this ache. In her brokenness, over time, she begins to pick up the pieces and take a few small steps onward. Many of us repeat deep experiences of love and loss over and over. With strength of heart and resilience of soul, we may hear an enduring voice, and this voice, once heeded, leads one onward differently. At least it was so for Psyche, and her voice helped me to hear and amplify my own.

First there is panic. At the moment when nothing seems possible, when she hasn't a clue in the world what to do next, Psyche panics. The loss, the pain, and the yearning are unbearable. As Joseph Campbell puts it, "This is the pain of being fully alive." She is disconsolate. She is on her own with nothing, seemingly, to live for. She is depressed and suicidal. She remembers the nearby river and drags herself there intending to throw herself in. As she peers into the rushing waters, she hears the most wonderful music. She turns around, and there before her is the cloven-footed god Pan playing his magic flute. This odd looking god, half man and half goat, fills her with sudden feelings of love and tenderness. So it was when she first saw Eros in the light of her lamp. It was then that she perceived the beast in the one she loves and felt the great music flowing from him into her even as he lay sleeping.

Ah, yes. Pan. Dancing, sensual, earthy Pan—the untamed male presence that refuses domestication. His wild spirit generates the desire for embodied knowledge and freedom. Pan is the pre-patriarchal masculine that Psyche needs to develop her inner balance. He is unconditioned masculinity. Comfortable being both a beast and a god, Pan is joyfully alive with the pulsing, thrusting energy of his body. He performs the music of the Earth as naturally as clouds dance through the sky. Pan has no agenda for Psyche. He wishes not to control her but rather to engage her in playful self-discovery. With irresistible music and dancing—*not with words*—he encourages both women and men to delight in the rapture of our senses including "the pain of being fully alive."

Pan lends his name to the word *panic*, and it is he who guides Psyche away from her suicidal moment. "Only the raging, shivering, shock of instinctive panic can break a woman out of the deadlock caused by trying to use masculine logic in an illogical, cruel situation," writes Mary Hugh Scott. Pan's masculinity is unconstrained by dulling dogma, rules, and regulations. His deeply instinctual logic is just what Psyche needs to transform panic into prayer. Prayer, he tells her, is the way to tune into the non-rational power of the self, and it is the first step towards mature selfhood. Prayer, Pan whispers to Psyche, is listening deep within herself. What an interesting irony it is that Pan and not some hooded ecclesiastic encourages Psyche to pray—and also that Psyche should meet Pan by the river in which she was going to drown herself. Prayer is a river to our deepest self. Here in the cathedral of the sensuous natural world, images of beauty and awe fertilize Psyche's open and vulnerable heart.

I have always loved Pan men—country boys and men who smell of the forest like my father, men who can use their hands to play music and build houses like my uncle. Sometimes they are Peter Pan men—which may leave something to be desired in the long run. In the short run, the youthful, spontaneous, carefree even reckless and often *irresponsible* natures (compared to mine) of Peter Pan men have helped me release the burdens of the world that I have carried since childhood. Pan men have brought the wind through the willows of my leafy past. They evoke the archetypal Green Man. Coming to life out of the shadows, such men have been delightful lovers, friends, lending their qualities and strengths to become those of my own inner life.

Feeling a *rightness* about Pan—his joyfulness, his music, the gleam in his eyes—Psyche becomes becalmed and begins to pray down by the river. Then, bearing offerings to each of their temples, Psyche entreats the gods and goddesses to speak to Aphrodite on her behalf. To a god and goddess, they refuse. Not that they don't empathize with her, but word has gotten out, and not a one is willing to do anything that Aphrodite could construe as being supportive of this upstart Psyche, a mere mortal.

Then it comes to Psyche what to do. This is really bold. Perfect in the only way I think life ever can be perfect—at a given moment, the right prompting comes from somewhere within. Call it Psyche's intuition or perhaps Pan's guidance, but something appropriate comes up.

Taking heart in hand, Psyche goes to the Great Goddess herself, Aphrodite. She begs for forgiveness and implores her to release beloved Eros so that Psyche and he may have their life together. This is the moment when mortal and goddess meet face-to-face, mortal female to divine female. Robert Johnson observes, "Psyche finally goes to Aphrodite's altar, for it is almost always the case that whatever has wounded you will be instrumental in your healing."

Aphrodite is at the top of her form, resplendent in her power, dripping in the shimmery wetness of her oceanic immenseness, and for the life of her, she can't imagine what Eros sees in this pitiful young woman who needs a good long week at a health spa. This is the moment Aphrodite has been waiting for, and she takes full advantage to denigrate Psyche, calling her a low-life, a real loser, not even close to being a match for her divine son.

Psyche takes it all in and doesn't flinch. She doesn't cry. She doesn't try to justify her actions or apologize. In a stunning moment, accepting her own worth as well as her own suffering, she withstands Aphrodite's tirade while feeling an inexplicable wave of hope mounting within.

What a great moment! Psyche confidently holds her ground. Aphrodite is impressed. She knows what courage Psyche has shown. There is no basis for Psyche to have thought she ever could have held her own with the Great Goddess. Yet she has done so, and with only painful, remnant memories of her love with Eros to sustain her. In that moment Aphrodite may get a glimmer of something in Psyche's mortal nature that excites, even thrills her. However, her fury is far from extinguished. She prescribes four tasks that Psyche must complete in order to win Eros back. If she fails any task, the penalty is death. These four tasks are as pertinent a recipe for soul-shaping for a woman entering the twenty-first century as they have been for our female ancestors through the millennia.

The tasks that Aphrodite prescribes for Psyche still strike at the heart of becoming an individuated, passionately alive woman—and they are instructive for understanding the development of the feminine in women and in men. For a mere mortal like myself, understanding what these tasks involved was a revelation, opening a doorway to comprehending what was happening to me. I became aware of archetypal forces at work in this story, and that something of what needed to happen in me also needs to happen in the world at large. As I deeply pondered these tasks, I was led onward in my journey to love and wholeness.

The deeper I entered this tale and took the tasks to be my own, the more I recognized the woman that had been pressing to be known, a woman who was ready to reclaim those joyful impulses I experienced when I danced in and out of the woods as a little girl. Yet, it was not my girlhood I longed to recapture, but it was rather the luminous and erotic light in the natural world and in my mature self.

Aphrodite summons Psyche the next morning and presents to her a mountainous pile of all kinds of grains and seeds. She commands Psyche to have them separated into their various piles by nightfall, then off she flies on her dove-driven chariot to a wedding festival. Thus, the first task is the sorting of the seeds, and of course, this could have been the last task. Certainly Aphrodite had every reason to believe it would be.

Again, Psyche feels overwhelmed, and thoughts of giving up consume her. Sorting all the seeds by nightfall is not humanly possible. Before she can gather enough energy to turn back to the river and act out the fantasy of throwing herself in, what should happen but the arrival on the scene of an army of ants. Immediately they set about to sort each seed into a pile of its own kind. With concentrated industry and efficiency, they complete the task by nightfall. When Aphrodite returns from the wedding, she's stunned and furious at Psyche. Sneeringly, she promises the next and far more difficult task in the morning.

This first task represents to me the great challenge of sorting out the expectations of others from the expectations Psyche has of herself. What is it others tell her she should need and want? What does *she* really need and want? Sorting conflicting expectations, feelings, and values is not an entirely rational endeavor. It requires invoking a rather primitive, instinctive capacity—an ant nature. Cultures inform women of many expectations, and generally do the sorting for us through customs, laws, and taboos. In relationships, the domain where many women naturally seek to derive a sense of identity and integrity, a woman's voice may be overcome by the voices of family, friends, or of culture at large. Her own authentic voice may be skewed or silenced. When a woman can rely on her instincts, her ant nature, she can better differentiate what it is she truly wants rather than what is expected.

At a moment of confusion and despondency, I experienced my version of a mountain of seeds looming before me. I felt that my acting career was slip-sliding away and with it my ability to make a livelihood doing what I love. Meanwhile my marriage moldered, and my biological Big Ben tick-tocked with a roar. I hardly knew where to begin.

"When a woman learns to stay with a confused situation and not act until clarity emerges, she has learned to trust the ants," writes Jean Shinoda Bolen, in *Goddesses in Every Woman*.

It's hard to pinpoint when the ants first arrived for me, but arrive they did, and when they did, some clarity began to arrive with them. It took a rather long time for certain mists of overly self-protective innocence to evaporate and for a new awareness to show a way out of some of the choices I had made for myself. Some of these choices had held such promise in the beginning, and many were fulfilled and fulfilling. Still, I had come to distrust myself, my way of being-in-the-world, so much that I could no longer hear my inner voice speaking what it was I really wanted or how I planned to get it. Did I have the courage to go after it? Wonderful friends and opportunities still enriched my life, but with my career and marriage in *transition*, and having no children or income, to put it daintily, my sense of self shrank. Without realizing it, I'd become eerily invisible to my self.

When a woman opens herself to her ant nature, she can sort through those things that distract her from seeking and obtaining her deepest longings. She can start to discern piles of seeds that are most important to her apart from those that are of lesser importance. The lesser seeds can then be swept away to make room for the more important seeds to thrive. The lesser seeds may be put in the pantry to be sprouted or planted later on. More often than not, in my case and in that of Psyche, the clarity of sorting allowed my instinctual voices to once again guide me.

With my new awareness, I did indeed learn more consistently to trust my own intuitive voice. In truth, I am a very intuitive person, and I have taken big and risky leaps that have turned out well. Yet events conspired in such a way that I was beginning to doubt I could make happen what I wanted to happen in my life. Feelings of failure began to eclipse my self-confidence. My ant nature did surface time to time, no doubt, but I had come, uncharacteristically, to dismiss them rather than to welcome them as instinctual helpers. Now I understand why they were hungrily hanging out on the kitchen counters. It wasn't just for the spilled honey. I became increasingly attentive to the synchronistic elements that were emerging bountifully. I have had other times in my life when this abundance of synchronicity bloomed. In fact, I feel now that it is always happening, but there are periods when we become more aware and attuned to synchronicity's munificence and omnipresence. Looking back, it seems that I began to leap towards things without knowing where or how I would land. Always these little ant-like helpers disclose my instinctual spirit. In so doing, they invigorate my ability to trust my decisions. One of these ant-helpers was a therapist, a man, who helped me remember the vibrant ten-year-old girl I once was. A passionate tree-climbing sprite was she who knew how to climb to high places easily for terrific views and the exhilaration. Why this man appeared at just this time in my life is the grace of synchronicity. It's hard to imagine a more gifted therapist for my particular needs. He had spent considerable time reckoning and wrestling with his own demons and issues. Years of therapy, he confided, had helped his feminine side flourish comfortably with his masculinity. His extraordinarily soulful adeptness reminded me of the tale of the fisherman told by Clarissa Pinkola Estes in *Women Who Run With Wolves*. The story is that of a fisherman who reels into his boat the skeleton of a woman. With a compassionate tear in his eye, the fisherman assists the woman in restoring her lost flesh. By means of the *tear of compassion in his eye,* as I experienced it in our work together, my therapist created the environment in which I could begin to reconstitute myself.

In another instance of synchronicity, a publisher interested in a manuscript I'd submitted sent me a catalogue of current publications. Among those listed, a book about women and relationships caught my attention—*Medea's Folly* by Tanya Wilkinson. I ordered it. Reading it I was impressed by how sensitively the author spoke about the inner world of women. For a moment I considered writing Wilkinson. I never did.

Fast-forward several months, my ant nature began rousing me with notions about going back to school to finish my undergraduate degree. Heeding these inner promptings, I searched for a place with an accelerated bachelor's program. I contacted a school I had read about much earlier, the California Institute of Integral Studies (CIIS) in San Francisco. The educational focus of CIIS is consciousness and personal transformation. Given my interest in the ways of the spirit and psychology, it seemed to be a perfect fit, and within a matter of a weeks, based mostly on feelings and intuition and without much thought, I decided to attend this school, flying from Los Angeles for classes once a month. Well, who should be among the faculty? Dr. Tanya Wilkinson.

During my second quarter, I had a free slot to do an independent study. I approached Wilkinson and asked about doing my independent study with her. She agreed. Initially, I had no idea what I could conjure up as a topic. It came to me almost overnight. Of course, I wanted to explore the myth of Psyche and Eros, and in accord with her background as professor and therapist with a Jungian perspective. The seeds of this book were thus planted.

Though a good student with top grades when I was younger, school had held little appeal for me. School was something I eagerly left behind, except when I had attended the Pasadena Playhouse on the road to being an actress. At CIIS, I was on fire with Eros, in all its many forms. Keeping the audio up on my inner voice found me leaping and seeking in the most zestful and stimulating ways. Many ant-like friends, classmates, and teachers, seed-sorters of the first water animated this new direction of my life. I was vitalized beyond all my imagining. Modeled after the visionary educational paradigms of Paulo Friere, the CIIS learning process is highly participatory and dialogical. I learned *how* to think rather than *what* to think. I was continually engaged with my eccentric, oddball, out of the box, and yet thoroughly sane in their ways cohort of all ages. Their provocative head-and-heart intelligence flung me into a more critically thinking and more fully integrated selfhood. I consider my decision to take up this form of learning and its profoundly energizing adventure to be a highly significant consequence of the sorting of my seeds.

The next task Aphrodite cooks up for Psyche is the gathering of the golden fleece. Pointing with haughty mien towards some rams on the far side of the river, Aphrodite demands, "Bring me the golden wool of those rams and be back by nightfall, or you will die." As Aphrodite flounces off to a game of croquet, Psyche looks across the river at the fierce rams munching in the field. This is really too much. What was she even thinking coming here? Her heart is breaking. She longs for Eros all the more, for the sound of his voice, his laughter, the smell of his hair, and the gentleness in his touch. She is struck with the folly of even imagining that she can obtain the golden fleece. Once again she heads for the river to end her life. Psyche is nothing if not dramatic. As she steps into the water, the slender green reeds at the water's edge whisper to her. Yes, they whisper.

They tell Psyche the secret to obtaining the golden fleece. The rams are very violent in the noonday sun, and to move about in their domain at this time of day, she would be battered to death. She must wait until the sun goes down. At dusk, when they quiet down, she can slip into the pasture and pluck the golden fleece safely and effortlessly off the bushes and brambles they have brushed against as they strolled by. And this, of course, is just what our plucky and grateful Psyche does.

As it strikes me, this task is about approaching dilemmas and dangerous situations indirectly, not assuming the confrontational stance of many masculine approaches. Still, the story of the golden fleece is a flat out scenario about how to take one's personal power. It emphasizes a woman's tendency to exercise her power without being like a man, without obliterating her femininity. There does not always have to be a struggle in the noonday sun with big-shouldered goats that could pin you to the ground with their horns behind their back. For a woman to get what she wants, she may do well to wait for an opening when the sun gleaming through the trees a certain way illuminates some options while eclipsing others. The feminine way of getting what one wants is less likely to involve slaying someone or destroying something. A woman's way to power often takes into consideration relatedness, opportunity, and timing. The direct route is not always the one she feels most comfortable with.

This second task and my reckoning with it have caused me considerable distress. The prevailing interpretations of this task emphasize a craftiness and cunning that I am not always comfortable with. In the past, I've usually had to find a "spiritually correct" way of doing things in order that I can think I've been the bestest, goodest girl in the world while winning an academy award and the Good Housekeeping Seal of Approval to boot. Being calculating had seemed to me like being deceitful. Yet I was also envious of that attitude affirmed by the proud father of the bride at the wedding mentioned earlier—namely, her confident ability to employ the same techniques and rationality used in the good old boys' network that pretty much dominates world cultures. It's quite a quandary and quite paradoxical, this idea of how to manipulate others for one's self interest without their knowing they are being manipulated, or in such a fashion as to invoke their mutual support and perhaps grudging respect.

Clarissa Pinkola Estes deals with these issues astutely. In her storytelling, Estes brings to light the haunted, hungering places in a woman's psyche needing personal development. It seemed to me that I'd avoided some of these power issues because of certain ideals I had. With the insights I gained from Estes, I was able to dismantle certain emotional and psychic scaffoldings I had been unable to let go of. What was appropriate to the younger woman was no longer appropriate and was in fact harmful to the person I was becoming. With Estes, I got a lot closer to the original *wild girl* I wanted to re-enliven and also to the *wise woman* I was hoping would emerge. I was after the "wise innocence" of the mature woman rather than the *naïveté* of the young girl.

Meanwhile, I had many assumptions to get beyond in order to become a *wildly* alive woman. I was uneasy embracing tooth and claw realities, reluctant to sniff the air for prey and predator or to become vigilant in ways that would require me to doff my rose-colored glasses. Refusing to "lower my standards" to be the earthy woman I was trying to be was presenting one heck of a self-contradiction. Taking power in such strong ways seemed to threaten the intimacy in my relationships. Plotting something secretively, cunningly, still gives me the heebie-jeebies, even when I sense I need to be protective of myself.

How do we hold onto our vulnerability, our fluid imaginings, our hearth and heart, if we wield the exact kind of power men have employed in our culture for thousands of years? Women not only need to learn how to take power but also to be clear and committed to the kind of power that makes sense to us down into our bones. Now let's consider another issue at stake with Task #2, one that has been a lot of hard work for me personally. Why should a woman have to take her power indirectly, surreptitiously? "Why can't she simply pin down the ram, take his fleece, and leave triumphant?" queries Robert Johnson in *She*. Johnson has no answer for this; neither do I. He feels this myth poses the question of how much masculine energy is enough or too much. Too much obviously causes great harm and trouble. There are moments, however, when the direct approach is the optimum one. When I feel an injustice has been enacted, I'm much more capable of confronting someone than being sideways about it. Perhaps that's when instinct and intuition surface again and again to guide us all.

That said, I feel prevailing paradigms which champion the taking of power at the expense of relatedness and undervaluing the feminine worldview are amongst the most pernicious aspects of patriarchy. Nothing is to be gained by reiterating these old patriarchal patterns. To end war and violence against fellow humans, animals, and the planet, we must find, respect, and honor alternative, feminine ways of resolving conflict and maintaining the health and happiness of the Earth and its soul. That's why meeting Pan has the impact it does for Psyche. This form of masculinity does not wish to put the world, women, or feminine musings and ways of dealing with things, under a monolithic thumb. Pan means *all*—all ways or avenues are possible openings for Pan.

As the twenty-first century unfolds, presenting us with monumental problems and challenges so complex and dire they hardly seem solvable, we need a *pantheistic* kind of spirituality that places us back into a world of living things with living voices. In her time of need, when adeptness at taking power is of the essence, Psyche is informed by the green voices of the reeds and by the fields of intelligence that Pan oversees. In *Natural Grace*, Rupert Sheldrake proposes that we think of soul in terms of fields. More fundamental than matter, fields *are* consciousness of the unified psyche and cosmos. Is it any wonder Pan, the god of the fields and forests, should quicken us again so we may see and hear ourselves and the world in ways we have forgotten? Taking power. Ah, yes, the big one.

Meanwhile back to the myth again, when Aphrodite returns from a winning day at croquet, she is astonished. Psyche has indeed succeeded in obtaining the precious golden fleece. Aphrodite explodes with her predictable vindictiveness. She's not going to fool around anymore.

The next morning Aphrodite spells out for Psyche what the third task requires—filling the crystal vessel. Aphrodite hands Psyche a crystal goblet and tells her that she must fill it with the pure, icy waters flowing from atop the highest mountain, and return it full. Or else. And we know what or-else is.

This is not just any mountain. This is the steepest, most gnarly piece of rock and earth Psyche has ever seen. From a crevice at the uppermost part springs a black stream that courses down the face of the mountain until it enters a cavern below and is taken back up again. This is the river of life and death. At the place where it emerges into the daylight, hideous dragons with flaming, flickering tongues are poised to destroy whoever would try to scoop this precious water.

At this point utterly numb, Psyche is way beyond rationally knowing what continues to propel her to complete these tasks. She just keeps moving and starts up the mountain with the crystal chalice. One thought does enter her mind. Where there isn't a river, the mountain will do. If she can't make it to the top and get the water, she will throw herself off. Thus she climbs slowly but steadily until she reaches the pinnacle and can go no further. She collapses, too tired to cry. So thoroughly spent is she that she doesn't at first hear the flapping of enormous wings.

Until now, the other gods have not intervened in Psyche's plight and perils. But Zeus has taken pity on his son Eros. Overall, he's had quite enough of Aphrodite's mood swings and her fickleness. Also, he's been impressed by Psyche's enormous courage and persistence. Few of the gods or goddesses have shown the commitment to love that she has. Out of immense respect for her struggle, Zeus sends Psyche his favorite eagle to help.

Accepting the eagle's instructions, Psyche climbs on his back and spreads her arms out across his huge wings. Off they go together, high into the sky where the water sparkles like stars in the night. Together, they weave in flight past the dreaded monsters. Psyche feels the power of the mighty bird. She is exhilarated. For the moment, they are one. Flying to the summit and source of the roaring waters, she reaches down confidently with the chalice and fills it to the brim with the luminous *aqua vita*. When they descend to the bottom of the mountain, the eagle gently deposits Psyche on the ground and with a knowing look in his penetrating eyes, flies off.

This third task encompasses the vastness of life. In *Knowing Woman*, a book I read many years ago, Irene Claremont de Castillejo proposes that feminine consciousness functions diffusely, whereas masculine consciousness tends to be more narrowly focused. By this modeling, the left hemisphere of the brain may be associated with the masculine tendency to perceive life in detail, bits and pieces; the right hemisphere, more feminine, processes the context and the wholeness of situations, and details may be obscured.

In *The Alphabet Vs. the Goddess*, Leonard Shlain offers his musings as to how the two spheres of our brains process information differently. Shlain's ideas have to do with the eye. There are two kinds of cells in the eye, rod cells and cone cells. The rod cells are associated with the right, female hemisphere of the brain, and help us see the broader outlines of the big picture and overall patterns. They are sometimes fuzzy as regards details. The cone cells are expert at seeing details. When continually activated by the linearity of the written word, the cone cells come to function as a defining lens. This is exactly the view a woman needs at times, this specificity, to compliment her diffuse vision, so that she can focus on details when she needs to.

There are times when women need eagle eyes. The eagle can see the smallest movement and detail from very high in the sky and has the ability of focusing single-mindedly on those details. That single-minded focus assisted the hunter in bringing home dinner. A woman, too, needs this capacity, to do one thing at a time, even as she holds the big picture within her. Psyche's third task represents a woman's taking of power without being overcome by the vastness of her encompassing vision.

Usually so much more at home in and with their emotions, women sometimes need to develop perspective by adroitly distancing themselves from wounding and troublesome situations. This standing back can allow a woman to detect patterns and details which can help her focus on whatever she needs to address, whatever is roiling to be changed, specifically where and when she can administer the chalice of healing waters. Perhaps she is the one who must drink from the chalice before she offers a draft to others.

To fly on the back of an eagle and see the world as only an eagle sees is an epiphany. For the first time in a long time Psyche glistens. Predictably, when Psyche returns and hands over the brimming goblet, Aphrodite goes into a white-hot rage. Hell-bent on Psyche's destruction, Aphrodite now delivers the ultimate task. She has no doubt, none whatsoever, that Psyche will fail to accomplish this task—it is a task gloriously foolproof.

As many Jungians, scholars, and revelers in the myth observe, the final task is one that is rarely attempted by mortals. This task is aptly called the descent into hell, and back—if one is lucky. Aphrodite commands Psyche to travel to the Underworld to fetch a portion of Persephone's immortal beauty ointment. The ointment is to be put by Persephone herself into a small pot with a tight fitting lid, and then placed in Psyche's hands. Psyche must then deliver the pot unopened to Aphrodite. To attempt this task is to embrace one's own death. As Psyche knows, even Aphrodite herself would not go down to the Underworld. "Why me? I don't need this. What in the world am I doing this for?" These are voices one might expect to have shrieked inside Psyche's head. The other tasks were tortuous enough, but now this! Yet, isn't that how it always is? The closer one gets to being more fully conscious, the greater the pull to regress, to give up, to push the unknown away. Psyche is so bone weary, she can hardly remember what it is that drives her. But she does remember that whatever it is that summons her to try to complete such impossible tasks is as important as life itself. In her book *The Goddess,* Christine Downing refers to the psyche wanting its "in-self-ness." I think Psyche wants her in-self-ness, and her need and quest to have Eros in her life prepares the way for in-self-ness to be hers.

How can she make it to hell and back? Psyche puts the pot in her pocket and walks around in a daze. No ants came to her, no gentle reeds speak to her, and nary an eagle is in sight. As she walks outside, a Tower appears up ahead. She heads for it thinking she will throw herself off the top. This is it. It really is more than a mortal woman can handle.

And then another extraordinary occurrence happens. As Psyche is ready to throw herself from the edge of the Tower, the very stones speak to her with some very intricate directions. She is to take yonder path choked with brambles down into the underworld. In advance, she is to put two coins in her mouth and take a piece of barley bread in each hand. When she passes a lame donkey driver who will ask her to pick up some kindling wood, she is to refuse. At the river Styx, she is to give Charon, the ferry-driver, one coin to ferry her across. In transit, she is to refuse the groping hand of a drowning man who will implore her to save him. On the other side, she will pass by the three women weaving the threads of fate and fantasy. She is to ignore them. At the gate to hell, she is to throw one of the pieces of bread to Cerberus. As his three heads fight, she is to slip in to the Underworld to meet Persephone and to obtain the immortal beauty ointment. On return, Psyche is to repeat the steps in reverse.

I associate this task with the refusal to fix, save, and rescue everything and everyone in one's life—particularly at critical junctures. One's *serving* may be compulsive or predicated on being approved of and an avoidance of or shelter from the dangers inherent in going after what one genuinely needs or wants. Another pitfall in obsessively serving others is a tendency to enable others to keep on repeating harmful, toxic and self-defeating patterns of behavior, rendering them weak and guilty rather than encouraging them to assert themselves on their own behalf. This can be protecting the server as well, often in some unconscious way, perhaps obscuring an implicit desire to control others.

Task #4 had my name all over it, lit up in neon lights! Serving just felt right to me. A woman is a nurturer who is supposed to find the meaning of life in caretaking. Not to excel at and delight in doing things that serve the wellbeing of others feels dreadfully wrong, if not disgracefully selfish to many women. We have been raised to feel good about ourselves if we are the giving daughter, giving wife, giving mother, and so on. In fact, being feminine seems inextricably connected to deferring to others. This nurturing song without end many women experience as the ground of their being. For others, however, giving birth to a painting or a poem, discovering a cure for a dreadful disease, or exploring the mysteries of the Universe as a scientist, may be more exhilarating and gratifying than being a mother to a child. Whether motherhood calls to a woman, or being an artist, or both, the archetypal wellspring of her feminine energy, if compulsively adhered to rather than consciously chosen, can actually bring harm to herself and to others.

Over the years, I think too much of my sense of self-worth came from being a caregiver. Care giving started early for me when I became a second mother to my younger brother. I was in my early 30s when my father, diminished by alcoholism and soon to pass away, told me that he would "be alright if he could come and live with me." I believed for many years that I could rescue him—if only I could find something for him to live for. *Dad, why don't you get back to doing your photography?* But alas, by then nothing reached him or ignited a spark in him.

To some extent my marriage extended this pattern when I felt a considerable pull to devote myself to filling my husband's particular emotional needs. During my "return to school years," I became the sole caregiver of my mother, a stroke survivor who never regained her ability to speak. In the wake of her massive stroke and its life-changing consequences and challenges, care giving took on new dimensions.

Thus I came to pay and continue to pay close attention to the directions of the mighty stones. Stones are weighty ancestors of the Earth, full of its creative fires, tensions, and concreteness. The coins placed in her mouth serve not only as fare for the ferry, but they also prevent her from talking. This is an age of much talky-talking. Talk therapy, talk shows, talking books, dolls, cows—you name it. We are saturated with our talk and the talk of others. I do feel much of this talk can be helpful and healing. Countless individuals have improved their lives through the safe space that therapy provides. Genuinely sharing our stories, our shames, our secrets, opens us to the common yet complex ground under all our feet. We seem to benefit by airing our closeted lifetimes of stuff that has burrowed within our flesh, festering over time into dangerous diseases.

There comes a time, however, when the talking can become vacuous and imprisoning. Sometimes the continual *talk* tethers us to places we need to leave, rather than returning us to the tides of life. In meditation, or simply in silence, a space may be created that allows one to go about one's daily life without continually reciting a rosary of wounds. Amazing insights can dawn if one is not always rehashing the past. Repetitious chatter can dam up things that when opened up to fresh air may be diluted like a thin mist and drift away. Going back to school after a year of therapy helped me to stop much of my inner chattering. I became busy learning new ways to experience and think about my life and the world.

Curtain up again on the myth: Psyche gathers up her courage and walks the bramble path down to hell, all the while keeping her eyes open for traps which could claim her attention, distract and deter her from her mission. Straightaway she stumbles upon that poor lame donkey driver. Well, unlike the Psyche of days gone by, she doesn't stop to help him. This man needs to learn how to pick up his own sticks. She's picked up enough sticks to build an entire fort. She would have told him to have a nice day, but she had those coins in her mouth.

Next, she comes to the Styx. Naturally, she can't cross over something like a river without encountering another obstacle—in this case, the drowning man. Her first impulse could have been to reach out and save him. However, she needs the barley bread in her hands to dissuade that ferocious three-headed dog around the bend. But it's more than that. Death is a part of life. It's not possible to rescue everyone who is dying anymore than one can rescue oneself from death one day. To everything there is a season, and in this myth anyway, this is the season for this man to die. Difficult as it is to pass him by, Psyche senses it is not her place to endanger her own life in hopes of saving someone whose time has come.

It's not difficult for me to imagine Psyche's emotions on this trip to hell where she encounters all those needy others whom she feels are looking to her. However, Psyche now carries the weight of her recent life experiences. The Tower has warned her not to be distracted along her path. The newly emerging Psyche senses how easily her attention is dissipated by continually being available to others.

In *The Search for the Beloved,* Jean Houston writes of this moment that Psyche needs to be more "consciously generous"—"This meddlesome attitude all too often wastes our time and stops our own life initiative, causing us to become experts in others' lives and dunces in our own." It is difficult for most of us, perhaps, to take responsibility for our own disappointments and heartbreak while managing to avoid interfering in the various outcomes of others' situations. In truth, as Houston suggests, a light shines into our own experience and into the world when we learn how to become consciously generous.

The three women Psyche passes further represent a woman's tendency to get deeply involved in other people's business. Relatedness is a cherishing gift of femininity to humankind. Without it, humanity would be more lost than we already are. That said, a woman's gift for relatedness is most fruitful when her involvement with others is not addictive, automatic, or a substitution for not addressing and attending to her own needs and creativity. Some of us spend a great deal of energy shepherding other people's lives as if we were Border Collies. We get so entrenched in the ups and downs of others, their intrigues and their dramas, that our personal growth is sidetracked and sometimes stunted. Perhaps we do this to uphold some idealized version of self, one in which we unwittingly entertain some sense of superiority, rather than facing our own real feelings of limitation, vulnerability, and imperfection.

Jean Shinoda Bolen says, "Whether it is a person who needs their company or comfort, or the attraction of an erotically charged relationship, until a woman can say no to her particular susceptibility, she cannot determine her own life course." During the year I was securing my undergraduate degree, various circumstances needed my attention, most notably my mother's. I was the only person in her life in any sort of daily fashion. Her needs at times overwhelmed me, fed my feelings of failure, and shook the focus I needed as a full-time student. I had to make decisions which she little approved of, and which felt uncomfortable to me, and I had to say and adhere to *No,* knowing her response sometimes could be volcanic. Stroke survivors swing between extremes. It's doubtful I could have negotiated the emotional turf between us had I been younger and not yet exposed to the sorting of the seeds and all the rest that Psyche has bequeathed.

So often during those times at school I felt I was letting someone down, or was remiss in some manner to address something needing my attention. Also during this time, my friends and I were not always available to each other as we were before new directions and callings overtook us. Even so, through all the changes we encountered, we remained friends. Somehow we weathered the territory of *birthing* different women from the younger versions of ourselves. Today we're just as crazy, mystified, and full of humor as we once were, but we are also wiser, more authentic, and more free.

In addition to women friends, it is extremely fulfilling for me to spend a great deal of time with my fella. Without a father around as I grew up, I had missed out on the sounds, the scents, the feelings, the confusions, and the touches of being around a man to bloom feelings in my body and soul that fuel me like nothing else.

Though relationships with both women and men are very important to me, I understood why Psyche was instructed to pass by the three women *weaving stories of fantasy and fate*. There are those times and places in life when and where one must travel alone, without the best of girlfriends, boyfriend or husband physically by one's side. Passing by all requests for her attention, Psyche finally arrives at the gate to Hell, throws some bread to feisty ole Cerubus, and walks into Persephone's queendom.

I recall Mary Hugh Scott's imaginative musings about Persephones giving Psyche a guided tour through the palace, past the rooms of remembrance that hold Psyche's hopes, desires, failures, and all the stuff that never came to pass—lost moments when love eluded her, occasions when she refused the call to risk something that was calling to her or to go after something dearest to her heart. I've walked through *memory rooms* like these in the past few years. I know the pain and sense of loss within some of them, and the joys and gratifications within others. These rooms are filled with dreams met and lived that continually stoked the fires of my enthusiasms, along with the dreams beyond my reach. Holding the bodies of stillborn possibilities, I have felt grief. I have also sensed something else. How even in my failure to achieve them, these inspirations gave me life and kept me looking forward. I could almost hear myself say, "Good bye, old beloved dreams. Thank you for the way you guided me even when you remained beyond my reach."

Dreams have such a cloud-like reality. One remembers the beauty of a cloud forever as it passes by, not as a single cloud but as the procession of all the clouds that appear and disappear. So it is with dreams. Like clouds they all pass by. There are always more clouds and dreams to come, to take your breath away, to make you sigh about loss, and to lead you to sing about the irrepressible way life continues to renew life.

Such are the rooms that disclose the power of the underworld queendom. Persephone knows how the demons reign and steal away life. She knows the secret to transforming bitterness, regret, and sadness into eternal life. For in the darkness of the underworld, just as in the dark, wintered soil of spring, new life is always waiting. As the regenerating source of the feminine principle, it is She, Persephone, who continually gives birth to new creations, She who brings a new person out of the husk of the old. She breathes life back into death pushing spring up through the hard, frozen, snowbound earth with a trumpeting daffodil.

Psyche might have been entranced by Persephone's awe-inspiring nature, seduced into remaining in the queendom of immortal life. How tantalizing to be this close to the mysteries of life and death. But Psyche had been through enough to sufficiently avoid the temptation to fall back into a sort of Sleeping Beauty slumber where nothing can harm you. "Many women who safely make the journey thus far fall into the trap of identifying with Persephone's mysterious charm. No further development is possible to them, and they remain a kind of spiritual fossil with no human dimension," says Robert Johnson.

There is something else to consider about this visit to the Underworld. Why does the beauty ointment come from below, from Persephone's domain—the place beneath, rather than the airy light from above? A response that comes to my mind concerns the difference between the hero's quest and the heroine's quest. Often in myths, a woman finds her deepest self and sovereignty by *falling* into something. Alice falls into a big hole to find Wonderland. Women tend to *fall into* their centers by *descending* into their feminine nature. Long before patriarchy co-opted and narrowed the imagination, initiates into the feminine mysteries were led down into the body of the Goddess who was the original image for the Earth and cosmos. The earliest creation myths involve a female being emerging from darkness becoming enfleshed. Both men and women refer to being enraptured by Eros as *falling* in love.

The hero's journey usually involves an *ascent*, a slaying of something, a conquering and overcoming of whatever exists as an obstacle to the hero's desires—vanquishing evil in some form. The masculine must emerge from the dark matter of the mothering Universe, no small enterprise when you consider physicists tell us that the Universe is mostly dark matter. From the lush, nurturing darkness of his own mother's womb, a male must emerge sufficiently to separate and actualize a dynamic force equal to hers. The hero must slay and/or dispatch that which keeps him from realizing *his* true nature. Yet if he also slays the feminine in himself he will need women in ways that may continually trouble him and the women that he becomes involved with.

For the feminine, the heroine's journey, at least at this time in *herstory*, centers in reclaiming the inexhaustible richness of her own, indigenous dark matter. *She* is her own home from the beginning, but she will need to journey nevertheless to fulfill her original and authentic self. She has lived too much and for too long in the ascendant masculine light, indeed enslaved and required to seek salvation from a kingdom in the sky, a kingdom from the neck up, of *man-made* ideals and ideologies. In the deep well of her being, the feminine is connected to the sweet smells of the Earth, of the soil, that are the nourishing perfume of her soul. In darkness emerges the feminine light from which all life in the Universe springs forth.

Psyche takes nothing from Persephone but what she came for, as instructed—the immortal beauty ointment. Once she has secured the pot with the tight fitting lid, Psyche thanks Persephone and is on her way. Her return to the upper-world is uneventful. She does everything that she was told to do on the way down in reverse. With hell behind her, she does something that changes everything. Having caught a glimpse of herself on the watery mirror of the river, she sees in her haggard face what all these tasks have taken from her—her youth and beauty. At last she is so close to being reunited with Eros. All she has to do is return the pot unopened to Aphrodite, and Eros will be returned to her. Instead, Psyche takes off the lid to try some immortal beauty ointment for herself.

Paradoxically, many construe this climactic twist, her momentous decision of disobedience, to be key to Psyche's eventual victory. This thrilling turn of events indeed sparks our spirits. Thus tempting the fates, her gesture of disobedience affects us as powerfully as it does not only because beauty is something we all wish for, but also because this quest for beauty is enfolded so deeply into the quest for love. Too often we resign ourselves to never sensing this beauty and great love in our lives—never having them.

The beauty that Psyche wishes to reclaim is more than physical, yet I personally have no problem empathizing with that longing for physical beauty. What woman doesn't want to be beautiful in herself and for the man she loves, to offer him beauty by her presence in his life. Eros—*a god!*—probably still looked fantastic. After all she had been through, Psyche wanted to equal him in every way. In *Amor and Psyche,* Erich

Neumann offers his interpretation that "In the beginning Psyche sacrificed her Eros-Paradise for the sake of her spiritual development; but now she is just as ready to sacrifice her spiritual development for the immortal beauty of Persephone-Aphrodite, which will make her pleasing to Eros." This is not regressive on Psyche's part, rather "By preferring beauty to knowledge, she reunites herself with her feminine nature, it is no longer the beauty of the young girl who sees nothing but herself, nor is it the seductive beauty of Aphrodite, it is the beauty of a woman in love, who wishes to be beautiful for the man she loves."

At the instant of accomplishing her passionate success, Psyche's choice, taking her risk, exposing her exquisite vulnerability, is possibly the most significant moment of the myth. Psyche's has been permeated with many elements of the *hero's* journey. She has acquired what she needs of masculine energy—she has sorted the seeds, she has gathered the golden fleece, and she has proved that she has eagle eyes when needed. All these she is willing to lay behind in order to possess the divine beauty of her wholeness and her womanliness. I couldn't agree more with Neumann when he finds that "A Psyche who fails, who for the sake of love renounces all principles, throws all warning to the winds, and forsakes all reason, such a Psyche must ultimately find favor with Aphrodite, who assuredly recognizes a good part of herself in this new Aphrodite."

If Psyche had obeyed Aphrodite and left the lid on, she would have perpetuated another double-bind: Sure, she'd get Eros back, but it would be at the price of being a *good* little mortal woman taking on a monstrous goddess-almighty mother-in-law. Now that Psyche has gone through what she has, Surprise! it's not worth it to have her beloved Eros knowing he and she will be all the more dictated to by his mom, the mother-in-law from hell; well, not *from* hell, but certainly intent on sending Psyche there if ever and whenever the urge might strike her. Both Psyche and Eros must take on Great Mother, to be fully developed. *We all must do this for our own selves.*

You have to admit this ragtag Psyche fresh from hell knows a thing or two about beauty and about Eros. It was beauty that set things in motion in the very beginning. Her mortal beauty had posed a threat to Aphrodite. Psyche's own beauty precipitated an odyssey that transformed her life, and now she has the power to restore and affirm that beauty in her own hands. No one has given that power to her. She found it in herself as anxiety stalked her down into the darkest trenches of self-discovery. *Why shouldn't she take some ointment for herself?* This she does. There is nothing detectable in the pot when she opens it, but invisible vapors instantly envelop and entrance her. Within moments she falls to the ground into a deep and deathly sleep.

This unflinching taking of power never fails to sweep me up. I value this moment which Psyche hands to us as much as any in this tale. Just writing about it, I feel my stomach flutter. For one thing, it scares me even now to think that I might not have taken some of that ointment. I might have obeyed, thinking I would be rewarded once again for being such a good little girl. I needed this moment as much as any in this tale to free me from my repressive ideas about *goodness*. The taking of the immortal beauty ointment involves bravery and consciousness, and most of all self-love.

Although she is exhausted, Psyche is fully aware of what she is risking in her desire to be beautiful for love's sweet sake. Perceptions of beauty have varied and do vary from culture to culture. Today it changes face almost every other week. Blue Mohawk hairdos and safety pins in the nose do it for some folk, but whatsoever is considered beautiful, beauty of any kind is hungrily sought as something numinous, divine. There is hardly a person alive, I feel, who would not hold that a star flooded night fills the heart with an exhilarating sense of beauty. When we see the stars, every cell in our body vibrates with star songs. Such beauty feeds, stirs, and allures each of us, as were our ancestors enchanted. Few would argue, surely, that at one time and place or another, this planet is one majestic landscape. In ways we can barely imagine, we organize ourselves, our lives, around this beauty. We long to be alluring along with the Earth and Universe.

Until this moment, Psyche has followed the advice and guidance of others as she has completed four life-threatening tasks. Now, Psyche intuits that she can and will use take this divine beauty ointment for herself. She will know its secret. It was not suffering and aging that had undone her. The hardness in her eyes and around her mouth was the result of constantly deferring and obeying. Psyche now understands that goodness as determined by others can at times be a false goodness. If the wholeness of a person is not somehow dealt with, ugliness and violence may rise up. Much of what is considered *the good* is repressive and destructive. After visiting the Underworld, Psyche has relinquished the final remnants of maternal and virginal ways of relating as being the preferred and primary ways of being feminine. She has also loosened her grip on needing to calculate all of life in terms of security and predictability.

A journey to hell and back reveals how very bound-together the world is by its terrors and its beauties. We try to deny the more horrifying aspects of reality at great peril to our own selves and to one another. The sacredness of life is its wholeness, its all-ness. Reality is the dramatic symphony of the enthralling and terrifying beauty of Everything. And ironically, most of Everything is still unknown to us. Psyche has been willing to face that unknown because somehow she has never lost a desire for a kind of love that in most mortal eyes, and even in the eyes of the gods and goddesses, is *impossible for mortals*. This is love composed of vulnerability and strength, joining the human and divine. The search for that love almost ends for Psyche when she wipes the beauty ointment across her weary face.

Mary Hugh Scott writes:

> *Whatever opens up or penetrates the unknown is beauty ointment. So it can be almost any pursuit that reconnects a woman with her creative ground, the part of her that is yet unknown— writing or singing or dancing or sculpting or playing the flute, or taking a vacation by herself or with her husband or with friends. By claiming her right to Persephone's immortal beauty ointment, Psyche could begin to live her life, rooted and grounded in her consciousness of the value of her own feminine being.*

Downing observes, "I think again of the beauty box that Psyche had to obtain from Persephone—clearly the beauty it provides is very different from any Aphrodite might have had the power to bestow." Not even Aphrodite can give Psyche the beauty of her self. That is something each woman and each man must realize individually.

Now Eros re-enters the saga. How is it that this is the critical moment for him to fly to Psyche's side and become her rescuing hero? Could he have heard the body of the woman he loved slump to the ground? To my mind, the reappearance of Eros at this moment indicates that he has gone through his own profound life changes. He realizes what Psyche has done to be divinely beautiful for him. It sinks in that during this entire journey to know her mortal self, she never lost her love for him. However it may be for a god, Eros becomes more conscious of a love even he didn't know he was capable of.

This story might not hold the charge for me that it does if Eros had not come to Psyche at this time. If she had awakened by some sheer force of will, or if some god or goddess other than Eros had intervened, Psyche's story would still be a powerful one, but not as redeeming a tale as it is. This is Psyche's story to be sure, but this is a love story, and love stories are all about *relationship.* This is the moment when Eros must assume a conscious and quickened maturity that he's been lacking. If he and his mortal beloved are to come together as equals, it is now Eros who must see Psyche for who she is. She has come to wholeness of self through a journey of epic transformation. Eros must take his journey as well. The conjoining of their journeys now becomes luminous in the fullness of maturity and mutuality. At this moment, after tasks that required intensive action, the time has arrived when Psyche needs to be receptive to the ministrations of Eros. There is passion, an active resonance, in passivity. Receptivity is as vital to deep relatedness as assertiveness.

"I am a woman who needs to be seen. I need it in a basic way, as in to breathe, to eat" is the opening line from *The Power of Beauty* by Nancy Friday. I imagine that this desire *to be seen* is intimately coiled up in the stardust which we came from and which we *are*. Perhaps a yearning is inherent in our *being*—to be seen, to be felt and experienced in our being-ness. There are philosophical grounds for understanding that that *feeling* persists in the thing-ness of everything. Eros can be understood as the very cosmic force, the feeling tone that is the individual soul and collective soul—*anima mundi.*

In *The Power of Myth*, the magical television series hosted by Bill Moyers, the great mythologist Joseph Campbell talks at length about the time of the troubadour. The troubadours were the singing poets of the twelfth century. They were pioneers in love, the first to think of love as we do now—as a person-to-person relationship with two lovers deciding to be the authors and means of their own self-fulfillment. The troubadours felt that Amor is a personal love, unlike Agape, which is impersonal. Amor was not love in general, but love for *that* woman or *that* man. The troubadours held this particular realization of love to be nature's noblest work. This is the beginning of the Western romantic ideal of individuals taking matters of love into their own hands— taking one's own experience as the source of wisdom. This was the gift the musical troubadours bequeathed to us. The best part of the Western tradition has been recognition of and respect for individuals.

Indeed, Eros must have initiated the move towards a love that would not submit to his mother's demands or shrink from her disapproval. Let's imagine that during that interlude while he was apart from Psyche, Eros wandered into the forest and met a troubadour, a man not emasculated by his culture, his politics, his religion—or his mother. There is an essential ingredient to being a troubadour; namely, one must possess a gentle heart, a heart capable of deep erotic love, not just lust. To Campbell, a gentle heart suggests one who is capable of compassion. This is just what Psyche needs from Eros at this moment, his compassion. The original meaning of compassion means to *suffer-with*, to *submit to suffering together*. While apart from each other, Eros and Psyche come to realize that wounds of passion can be healed only by means of the instrument that brought about the wound. That is, only love can heal the absence of love.

With a gentle heart and deepened soul, Eros flies in great haste to his beloved Psyche. When he sees her on the ground, he alights beside her and lifts her limp body into his arms. Once again the utter strength of her vulnerability pierces his heart. As tears of recognition slowly trickle down his cheeks, he wipes the deadly vapors from her face. Instantly, she opens her eyes and gazes into the face she has seen only once before. In that moment, for the first time, Psyche and Eros see each other in full recognition of what is uniquely *their own*. Eros smothers Psyche with kisses as she weeps with happiness. After their unbearable separation with its loss, loneliness, and uncertainty, they rock back and forth in each other's arms as joy cascades through their re-united being.

The pot is brought to Aphrodite. If she knows it's been opened she elects to say nothing. Eros flies to Zeus to petition for *goddess-hood* on behalf of his beloved. The request is granted. A marriage is planned, a wedding feast rivaling the most sumptuous celebrations for which Olympus is famous.

As stars come out, mandolins strum and night birds rustle in the trees, Aphrodite, flush from dancing, stops for a telling moment and looks across the dance floor. She watches her son Eros and the remarkable woman he has married, a mere mortal woman whom she pushed to the limits. I picture Aphrodite's golden light fanning out unto the sky, her alluring depths magically transporting all who look upon her everlasting loveliness. As she watches the dancing young lovers, now husband and wife, Aphrodite smiles, warming the chilly night air. She is *divinely* pleased with herself.

I prefer to think Aphrodite hoped all along that Psyche would prevail. I think she perceived in Psyche a mortal capable of embodying what she has always known and embodied. That knowing, as Downing observes of Aphrodite, is that "In your realm sensuousness and consciousness cannot be severed from one another." I further like to imagine that as Psyche whirls around the dance floor, her body close to Eros, she looks over his shoulder and sees in Aphrodite the limitless passion for life that is now her own. She had not known such passion before meeting Aphrodite. I imagine their eyes meet, and when they do, the light they bring forth together will warm all lovers everywhere and always. Though they may never speak of it, they know their relationship has recovered and redeemed the lost love humankind is looking for.

In my fantasy, Eros presses his face into Psyche's hair, into her shoulder, nuzzling her ear while singing snippets of *Time After Time* that the orchestra is rendering. He reaches down to caress her belly where new life is growing and whispers in her ear something that is only theirs to know. She throws her head back in laughter. He takes her by the hand, whisks her off the dance floor, and carries her up to a sumptuous bower lit with scores of candles from Pier One—always a good place for candles. They giggle playfully as he struggles with her extra girth, and I hear him say to Psyche, "If it's a girl, Darling, I'd like her name to be Pleasure."

Psyche, her heart glowing like a ruby, says, "Pleasure. Hmm? I was thinking maybe Bella, but yes I like that."

So Pleasure—Joy—is their child's name, for as we know, that is the land from whence she comes.

The story of Psyche and Eros became my soul map, a legend for understanding the changes I was reckoning to bring about in my life. The myth continues to disclose and bring forth life from that dark matter, the unknown, which shapes all our lives. There is so much in Psyche I cherish. I love her for all the ways she helped me. I am emboldened by the strength she continually finds in herself every time she is about to give up, and I am enriched by the sublime vulnerability she never loses along the way. By allowing herself to be capable of being wounded, she was able to be receptive to the wholeness of her Self. As Maureen Murdock writes, "It is the job of the heroine to enlighten the world by loving it, starting with herself."

Refuse to be passive, Psyche tells us. When you are willing to risk everything for love, the most astonishing transformations happen. Believe in yourself, in love, in pleasure, in the gifts of your maturity. Always listen for the voices of the reeds, ants, eagles, stones, and rivers. Nature is the greater Self, calling you to the abandoned longings of your soul and the fullness of your being. Remember, says Psyche, your senses are the sacred thresholds of the body that serve as portals to divine and human love. They are there for you to experience life fully, sensuously. For divine and human love merged as one become the meeting place between Heaven and Earth where *more* is always revealed and what is lost is regained.

Lest we think the tale of Psyche and Eros to be merely of another time and place and not relevant to the struggles we are encountering every day, I suggest Psyche and Eros have never been more pressing for our consciousness than they are today in their mythic power to transform and give our lives meaning. They urge each of us to attempt the risks they took—that have helped us survive to the present day. We are all the daughters and sons of Psyche and Eros.

In *The Universe Is a Green Dragon*, cosmologist Brian Swimme urges:

> *Fall in love, as deeply as you can. That way the Universe becomes your primary teacher. We learn about love by falling in love.... Remember that the desire to make us over into love permeates the Universe. We are initiated into love when lured into the intense pursuit of the enchanted lover. If the initiation is long, and filled with doubt and suffering, the learning takes hold deeply.*

EPILOGUE

Psyche, Eros—and All of Us

The main advantage of this myth (Psyche and Eros) is that it speaks to all times, and so to our times too when the need of the soul is for love and the need of eros is for psyche.

—James Hillman, *The Myth of Analysis*

Prior to completing my text in 2000, I found myself at a crossroads. This can be notoriously confusing and unsettling, of course, with crossroads pointing as they do in multiple directions—north, south, east, west, left, right, forward, let go, hold on, do less, do more. Without realizing it at the time, I unstuck myself by following Yogi Berra's advice, "If there's a fork in the road, take it." That I did. I sallied forth—and went back to school.

Two weeks after graduation from California Institute of Integral Studies, I began graduate work at the Pacifica Graduate Institute outside Santa Barbara. Another unique locus of scholarship, Pacifica houses the archives of mythologist Joseph Campbell, as well as the archives of depth psychology luminaries Marion Woodman and James Hillman. Sure enough, with synchronicity still running strong, in one of my first classes, we took up the myth of Psyche and Eros.

During the next eight years the world of myth opened like a strange and exotic new flower. The professors at Pacifica are as brilliant, eccentric, and intoxicating as those at CIIS. Some of them have sacrificed tenure at other universities to be part of the iconoclastic musings Pacifica encourages. From every arena of life—teachers, psychologists, policemen, architects, engineers, writers, filmmakers, corporate executives—my classmates, many already having graduate degrees, wished to enhance their prior education and enrich already established professional lives. Many of us were over forty. A woman in one class was eighty; she flew from the East Coast once a month to attend classes. The small and exquisite campus, former estate of the Fleischmann family of margarine fame, bounded by the breathtaking Santa Barbara mountains to the east and the glimmering Pacific to the west, hosts a transforming magical mayhem, alongside serious and challenging scholarship.

The beauty of Pacifica is inseparable from its scholarship. A favorite moment came at day's end when dozens of little bunnies hopped out from the lavender bushes and feasted on the green lawns in the fading lavender light. This always brought me back to my senses and out of my head. Aphrodite's spell oozed in every shrub, oak tree, passing cloud and mountain shadow. Each time I was on campus, I had the feeling of falling in love with the place all over again. In *The Myth of Analysis,* a book collecting his essays concerned with the primacy of the Psyche and Eros myth in our time, Hillman writes "Beauty is the first attribute which draws Eros to Psyche.... Perhaps now we may realize that the development of the feminine, of anima into psyche, and of the soul's awakening is a process in beauty."

It's been a provocative odyssey revisiting the person I was fifteen years ago when I finished the Psyche and Eros text above. The world and I have been altered in many ways in the years since the end of the twentieth century. And yet the personal and collective patterns and archetypal energies that in-formed my world of fifteen years ago, and which thousands of years ago shaped the world of ancient Greece, still impart their influences in our individual lives and in world life. What does this mythic tale have to offer for us in the twenty-first century? How do Psyche and Eros survive amongst the accelerating pace and changes in our lives today? Fifteen years ago 9/11 had yet to plunge the American soul into horror, fear, and heartbreak. At that time my husband and I had one cell phone between us, a bulky piece of technology that we only used for emergencies. How do Psyche and Eros manifest in the cyberspace environment when each of us can communicate in an instant the most immediate and often miniscule details of our lives to the entire world?

As I look back on this work, I feel how the influence of the Psyche and Eros myth endures in my life unmistakably. I find that I continually use the psychological lens this myth provides. How is it, I wonder, that Psyche and Eros visit individuals who meet and sustain relationships, romance, and friendship over the Internet? How can Psyche and Eros thrive without the touch, scent, or taste of one another? Are we really more connected to and more erotically alive with one another through Facebook, YouTube, and Twitter—or are we getting more and more clever at keeping our physical and psychic intimacies and emotions at a distance?

For the past several years, many Americans have strained with bootstrap spirit to pull the myth of the American dream out of the clutches of a soul-crushing Great Recession. Millions around the world are also struggling with the Global Economy. Where are Psyche and Eros in our macro-economics—on Wall Street, in the corporate world, in the workplaces that are critical in of all of our lives?

How are our psyches faring as climate change sweeps across the planet with extreme weather— tornadoes, floods, and droughts? How do our psyches metabolize an earthquake and mega-tsunamis triggering multiple nuclear meltdowns? The Earth's soul is *our* soul. All these planetary extremes are resonant with Psyche and with Eros. Over the past twelve years, all life on Earth has become vastly more complex. The magnitude of Complexity itself has become part of what ails us, what withers our enthusiasm and confidence that personal, national, and global problems are in some way *solvable*.

Considering how much Eros sprang from every aspect of my return to school, I wonder where is Psyche and Eros in education, from the early years of learning, right on through university studies? Eros is rarely respected as being a vivifying component of education. In the classroom

Eros is generally suspect and suppressed. In *Teaching to Transgress*, the renowned educator Bell Hooks addresses the importance of Eros in education:

> *Understanding that eros is a force that enhances our overall effort to be self actualizing, that it can provide an epistemological grounding informing how we know what we know, enables both professors and students to use such energy in a classroom setting in ways that invigorate discussion and excite the critical imagination.*

When the myth of Psyche and Eros first entered my life, I reflected on the more private dramas of my own life and in the lives of those in my circles. Now I am contemplating what is happening in the world at large. And again, I feel overwhelmingly that the myth of Psyche and Eros is as relevant as ever. Even more than I imagined fifteen years ago, I believe the quest of the soul for Eros and of Eros for psyche resides at the very core of our lives. It is ever more apparent to me that the grand adventure between Psyche and Eros, these archetypal realities, creates the most real place of our existence.

After eight years at Pacifica, I had earned my masters and doctorate in mythology and depth psychology, something in my wildest imagination I had never entertained. My dissertation, *Singing: Soul's Mythic Mirror*, explored the musical etiology of the ancient myths that were often referred to as hymns and songs—*The Homeric Hymns, The Bhagavad Gītā (The Holy Song)*, the five-thousand character Chinese hymn, *The Tao Te Ching*. Myth, I theorize in my dissertation, is a musical way of peering into, mirroring, and telling stories about the realities of a Universe composed of musical frequencies and musical patterns on sub-atomic scales. Singing was probably our indigenous language, and even now singing is sometimes the only way we can say what we deeply feel. I suggest that myth is the music that composes the language of our soul—and its truest history.

At Pacifica, I also learned a great deal more about Dionysus. Among all the gods, he is the great lover of women, of the feminine. Dionysus *loves* Psyche. He is also Olympian founding father of the theater. I realized something that had never really occurred to me, which is that acting is inextricably involved with *acting out* various mythic archetypes that are subsumed in each and all of us. This is evident in the Greek passion for theater. Acting provides a safe and creative psychic space to explore the various characters and *creatures* that compose our personalities. An actor's profession allows for, in fact, usually demands that an actor access some of the less prominent personalities in herself or himself. In the earlier years of Hollywood, however, this was not encouraged. Movie stars became popular for exemplifying a singular persona, a single archetype—the love goddess, the Earth-mother, housewife, the swashbuckling hero, and the loner cowboy. It's called typecasting, but it could be called archetypal-casting.

Musing about archetypes in acting, I recall my mother saying that she marveled that I got such good reviews playing roles that *weren't like me*. Lady Teazle in *School for Scandal*, is a case in point. "Deanna McKinstry's Lady Teazle is brilliant. She braves her role as the unthinking, tasteless young wife of Sir Peter like water rushing over a fall—reveling in the unexpected turns of character, helpless to hold back. This is an actress who believes, and believing transports us to her realm." Lady Teazle was pure joy to portray and extremely easy for me to access. Whoever knows what archetypes lie slumbering barely beneath the surface of one's more well trotted-out personalities?

Around the time I was completing the Psyche and Eros text, I unexpectedly found myself again taking up an archetypal role in a vastly engulfing and exhausting saga with my mother. For the final ten years of her life, I was her sole caregiver. When still living in Boston, she experienced a massive stroke that initially left her paralyzed. Physical therapy and some good fortune rid her of the paralysis, but even after years of therapy, because of apraxia, her kind of speech impairment, she was never again able to speak. For almost seventeen years she was speechless. The first seven of those years she was able to stay in Boston and to live alone rather well. Eventually, loneliness and isolation eroded the quality of her life, and, with the help of the gods, I was able to put things in place and bring her to California.

The loss of her voice changed her and our relationship. The continually escalating demands of her situation, her diminishing neurological capacities, her lack of sovereignty and independence, our role reversals, and hard-to-call decisions, took us both to the underworld many times. I can barely imagine what it must have been like for her, imprisoned in her thoughts without the ability to express them. She was brave, plucky, downright heroic, and at times she was her familiar loving and happy self, especially glad to be with me and around our dogs. But alas, her rage could be Herculean. She had always been a good screamer, and her outbursts achieved titanic heights—which got me thinking a great deal more about voice, given that voice has been central to all the core interests in my life as actress, singer, writer, lecturer and storyteller. Mother still had a *voice*, and quite a dramatic one. What she had lost were all those things that come to life through the delicacies and joys of *speaking*.

As I cared for my mother, I pondered how the myth of Psyche and Eros draws us to be distinctly attentive to the voice of the feminine. The beating heart of this myth, in fact, is the value of the feminine, the feminine voice, and the status of women. During the final years with my mother, it was driven home how little value is put into caretaking, a role usually filled by women, and a role that is commonly unrecognized and devalued. Thus was the situation in our household and in many households.

The Greek word for household is *oikos*, the root of the word *economics*. As the myth unfolds, Psyche and Eros long to meet in each of our households and homes. And what about our communal home—the Earth, the Big She? Joseph Campbell once remarked that perhaps the new and most powerful mythic image of the past several decades, the image that unites every creature, person, and living organism on this planet, is the photo taken from the moon of the blue, blue Earth swaddled in swirling white clouds. This image of home, the Earth, where Psyche and Eros find each other amidst chaos, joy, and heartbreak, stirs us deeply, and any new mythology must carry this unifying image of our earthly home.

Today, climate change is re-arranging our planetary home. Extreme weather is shifting, pruning, and trimming the land and its inhabitants in alarming and irrevocable ways. Humans have contributed egregiously to these changes, in part by making choices that value masculine fantasies about how to live life at the expense of choices favoring nurturance, connection, and cooperation. Grievously, most corporations worship the bottom line and are concerned with profit, the accumulation of money as an end in itself, rather than with the well being of Mother Earth and all living things. We see around us the consequences of degrading those values that are more aligned with the feminine aspects of our nature. Home foreclosure is a deeply wounding reality in our times.

Hillman feels the psychological material contained in the myth of Psyche and Eros holds redemptive grace for the disturbances of psyche and world life that persist from the twentieth into the twenty-first century. He traces much of the distress that has brought so many of us into therapeutic settings to the devalued and even despised feminine. Hillman contends that the inferior status assigned to the feminine and traits often considered pejoratively to be feminine—weakness, gentleness, softness, hysteria, depression, vulnerability, and darkness—submerges a quality of consciousness that has by necessity gone underground, into the unconscious. Meanwhile, our whimpering, heartsick psyches quest for Eros. "We have been looking for love for the soul," Hillman says. As the song goes, we may at times look for love in all the wrong places.

Is the world a better place for women than it was a century ago, or fifty years ago, or even than it was fifteen years ago when I first entered Psyche and Eros' domain? Here in America, opportunities exist for women beyond those that were available during my mother's era, or even when I was a young girl. With the rising number of women walking through the doors that are now open to us, appreciation of the feminine would appear to be on the rise. But is it? If we look around the world, if we watch the news and read the newspapers, incalculable atrocities against women continue. Millions of girls are compelled to undergo circumcision, forced to become eight-year-old brides and bear children, trafficked for sex, or remain in bondage and sexual slavery. Even here in the U.S., where things are brighter for most women, Facebook's COO Sheryl Sandberg, in a commencement address at Barnard College noted: "As men get more successful and powerful, both men and women like them better. As women get more powerful and successful, everyone, including women, likes them less." We may indeed have "come a long way, Baby," but clearly there is a long road still ahead of us.

As I have revisited this 2000 text, it comes to me that we don't attend the theatre or the movies to watch two hours of angels having a nice conversation about how very nice everything is, especially the weather, with no bumps in the road, no dangers, no cliff-hanging conflicts. We want what soul wants—Eros, authentic and undiluted, and we crave the way Eros compels us to feel and experience life with a terrifyingly vulnerable sense of adventure even as it makes life so insane and messy. In other words we crave the wisdom and illumination that must come from the darkness we encounter, one way or another, on the road to find out what life is all about. We do well to keep in mind that great portion of the Universe that is dark matter. Dark matter deserves a little respect since it is as vital to creation as light.

You may be wondering where life has taken me regarding career, motherhood, my marriage. After all, these were pivotal concerns ruffling the feathers of my life fifteen years ago, concerns that drew me so potently into the myth of Psyche and Eros. Not becoming a mother has been a deep disappointment and loss. Many of my friends are grandmothers now, showing up at recitals, scheduling yearly trips to Disneyland, tilling the turf of their grandkids' lives with a great deal of wisdom, humor, and verve. While I think little is more important than being a good parent, or grandparent, I do feel there are expressions in and of life that can be just as meaningful and important for a woman as childbearing. Giving birth to ideas, music, art, scientific endeavors, all of these can be and are sources that provide a fecund and fervent meeting place for Eros and Psyche. Creativity flows and flourishes in endless ways. As sad as I can be about not being a mother, I'm grateful that my husband and I bring forth artistic creations, as is said of William and Catherine Blake, "with bright fiery wings."

I had the good fortune almost twenty years ago to meet one of the most remarkable individuals I've ever known—Laura Archera Huxley, writer, therapist, and widow of Aldous Huxley. Her friendship irradiated my life. She was doing a headstand at her Hollywood Hills home when we first met. At eighty-three she had remained seductive, endlessly inquisitive, full of energy and exploration, more beautiful it seemed than when she was younger. Among Laura's significant accomplishments was founding an organization named *Children: Our Ultimate Investment.* What a lush embodiment of Eros and Psyche she was, although I didn't realize that at the time. What I did realize is that everything about her fascinated me, especially a passionate courage to be her own unique self. I never once felt she was inclined to be the good little girl. So many of us were drawn to her because she enlivened something in each of us that needed more energy and prominence in our own lives. Early in 2007, the year she passed away at ninety-four, she came to our home in Sherman Oaks for a singing lesson with my husband. Wearing a scarf I had brought her from China, looking every inch as beautiful as you might imagine Tinkerbell to be in her maturity, she entered our sunny living room with the grand piano and said, all fluttery and excited, "I'm as nervous as a school girl." That's how I want to be at ninety-four! Excited as a schoolgirl, full of Eros, taking a singing lesson.

During those years of my studies and caretaking my mother there was scant time to miss what had filled up my life since childhood—acting and singing. Occasionally I had opportunities to sing at both CIIS and Pacifica. Among the more fascinating of these opportunities was one that arose with Esther Hutchison, a Pacifica colleague who became a close friend. A beautiful woman, mother, and now grandmother, Esther's background is in the corporate world, counseling and heading leadership seminars with her husband, Morgan McCall, author and corporate consultant. Esther felt that the two of us had the right backgrounds to create a performance piece that combined theater with mythology. *Eavesdropping*

On Olympus portrays the various strengths and liabilities of the gods and goddesses such as they are played out through individuals in corporate situations. We had barely scoped out a rough outline of our Satyr play when we had a stunning opportunity to take it to China for a global economic consortium. It was a big success, and traveling to China was the trip of a lifetime. We experienced the Old China with its soup kitchens on the street and stinky hole-in-the-ground bathrooms, up against the New China, mobilized and as brilliantly lit up as any Las Vegas boulevard. We found old mythologies mingling with new mythologies, a nation moving quickly and boldly into the twenty-first century. We continue to perform *Eavesdropping* today in corporate settings and other venues.

I lecture at conferences, for therapists, at Jungian centers, about singing and why and how it is indispensible to our health, to growing new neurons in the human brain, to perceiving and being fully who we are. Music allows us to utter vociferously, to speak from our heights and depths—our rage, heartbreak, sorrow, grief, joy, and delight. Singing allows us to be who we really are, and who we really are is music. Small wonder the most successful shows presently on TV are those involved with singing and being a singing star. We all want and need to sing!

After an absence of over eighteen years, I recently returned to the stage in *Body Awareness,* a play by Annie Baker, an internationally recognized, young playwright, and directed by Conrad Selvig at the Cherry Center in Carmel. I played a PhD professor of psychology who has organized a conference touching on "women's issues," just as I was completing this epilogue—a genuine synchronicity!

A year later, at the PaperWing Theater in Monterey, I played the role of Violet, the mother, in Tracy Lett's Pulitzer Prize winning play, *August: Osage County.* With standing-ovation direction by Koly McBride, Violet, a wounded, wounding matriarch, took me to darkly challenging territory as an actress. Wearing my late mother's robe and slippers, incorporating the slippery-slopes and wobbly walk of her stroke, surprisingly, I found Violet difficult to leave behind when the play ended. It felt as if in some way I was responsible for her, as I had been with my own mother.

In yet another dollop of synchronicity, I was offered the opportunity to teach a class on Ecopsychology for the Viridis Graduate Institute, which offers the world's first Ecopsychology degree programs. During the time I completed my undergraduate work at The California Institute of Integral Studies, one book roused me deeply, *Ecopsychology; Restoring the Earth, Healing the Mind*, a series of essays edited by Theodore Roszak. These essays spoke to the pressing need of re-connecting individuals to the natural world. Healing ourselves of whatever ails us is inextricably concatenated with healing our destructive relationships with everything considered to be "other," including the Earth.

So enthused was I with the insights of this book, that I looked about for a school at which to pursue Ecopsychology. At the time, there was nothing available. Praise be, a year ago, Professor Lori Pye, PhD, a visionary with an extensive academic and activist background in environmental research, activism and study, founded The Viridis Graduate Institute, and we connected. We'd met a few years earlier when I presented a talk at a seminar that she organized on violence at my alma mater, The Pacifica Graduate Institute. The myth of Psyche and Eros opens provocative and revealing territory for connecting individuals to the silenced, muffled voices of the earth and all its creatures. And so once again, I was carried into its depths.

I am working on two one-woman shows, one involving America's earliest music and what it reflects about the American dream. In my mind, there is no country as mythic as America, the only country I know that is known for *having* a dream! Although this dream surely does not pan out for everyone, as Jean Houston remarks, "A myth is something that has never happened yet is happening all the time." With another initiative, I am rendering Psyche and Eros into a storytelling theatrical piece. In other words, I've come full circle to many of my original intentions and dreams. Who knows how they will play out? As actor Alan Arkin remarks in *An Improvised Life*, his original and wise memoir, "It's all improvisation." One is continually making up life as one goes along, with the materials at-hand, whether we like it or not.

Surely we have to consider that Eros might not have rescued Psyche from the cliff. Her destiny could have been to end up with Thanatos, the god of death. That's always happening among us. But my experience in the orphanage where I, too, felt abandoned as Psyche must have felt on the mountaintop, came with a strong message that I might be delivered back into life and loving hands once again. That's how myth can also play out, with Eros continually emerging even after the most devastating heartbreaks, delivering us deeply and vulnerably into the mysterious embrace of life—and Psyche is always, always looking for her beloved.

And that brings me back to the divine and mortal marriage between Psyche and Eros such as it has been manifest in the romantic improvisations of my own life and marriage. In *The Theater of the Imagination,* Clarissa Pinkola Estes, speaks of the many deaths that occur in a marriage. Death feels so distant from love, and yet death is tied so closely to love. In the thirty years we've been together, Rob and I have survived many disappointments and deaths. Woven amongst them have been endless blessings, much good fortune, lots of laughs, lots of troubles, lots of arguments, the best of heady adventures and opportunities, exquisite friends and the painful passing of friends and beloved animal companions, sublime scenery, therapy, five dogs, a cat, several homes, crossroads and crosshairs, and music, musicians, and singers. And love.

As to the whole kit-and-kaboodle of love and marriage, I've been asked more than once how Rob and I have managed to stay together. Sometimes I think I have a clue or two. Sometimes I'm quite mystified. I wish I had a recipe, but I don't. Showbiz does tend to pump up the volume on life, but in more ways than not, showbiz is very much life-biz, with perhaps a few fringe benefits—and perils. Trying to stay tuned and alive and compassionate, that is to say, suffering with passion, with another person for a long time, is surely among the most sacred, mysterious, and arduous adventures of life. Perhaps, it is *the* adventure. Knowing what I know now, and don't know, I could never presume to explain how a marriage can be sustained. However, I think the myth of Psyche and Eros offers us some provocative clues. And like all myths and parables, it is open to interpretation.

I am completing this writing in the place where I was first introduced to the myth of Psyche and Eros—in Carmel, among the most breathtakingly beautiful spots on Earth. We live here now. How's that for synchronicity! It still amazes me that we've been able to pull it off. The tempestuous and feral landscape of the central coast of California is gaudy with beauty and tends to bring out the poet in everyone who comes here. Scabrous cliffs, ocean-slaughtered ravines, elevating headlands, pelicans, seagulls, sandpipers, and all manner of seabirds and sea life hold daily dialogues with the sublime treats and terrors of the wind, and the brawling, bountiful Pacific. It is a requiem of light, transient mist, and fog.

Nestled within this mercurial music of sky, mountains, headlands, and forest is the tiny, quaint, and relentlessly picturesque Hansel and Gretel village of Carmel-by-the-Sea. Multitudes visit here. The energetic air whisks visitors down the main street of Ocean Avenue into glamorous shops and enticing restaurants. In its own way, Carmel is as mythic a place as Hollywood, and equally brimming with eros. Carmel has long attracted those who cannot resist its extreme beauty including many glamorous denizens of Hollywood. In 1914, nearly a century ago, renowned poet Robinson Jeffers and Una, his beautiful wife, arrived in Carmel. Viewing the scenic bluffs from their stagecoach, they felt they arrived at their "inevitable place." Their erotic relationship matched the eros of this place that became their home. Joseph Campbell arrived in the 1920s to befriend John Steinbeck and Ed Ricketts. Ricketts inspired Campbell's thinking that myth arose from the biology of the body. Also inspired by Jeffers' poetry, Campbell stated that the central coast was where his thoughts about mythology took root and began to coalesce.

Carmel still allures artists of all kinds, even with the display of excessive wealth. Finding a cottage an artist can afford pretty much comes under the heading of a fairytale, but as we know, fairytales can come true sometimes. Benefitting from the current recession, Rob and I, with our two English Setters, Asher and Winnie, moved here in 2008. Among the many draws to Carmel is the love of its inhabitants for dogs. *Dog Fancy* magazine—yes, be impressed—named Carmel the Most Dog Friendly Town in the USA. There are dog menus in restaurants, water bowls and biscuit-baskets on the street, dog friendly inns with dog bedding and gourmet goodies for Fido in one's morning breakfast hamper. On the heavenly white sands of Carmel Beach, Calder, another English setter who entered our lives when our beloved Asher passed away, and Winnie frolic, chasing and, thankfully, never catching seagulls and their shadows. After dogs, the other reigning life forms in Carmel are the omnipresent trees. Rather than forcing the removal of trees, streets wind around them. Dogs and trees rule, and that makes for a very sane, egalitarian system to my fey mind.

We found a small home with a separate studio where Rob teaches when he is not in Los Angeles where he retains a large clientele. When he's teaching in Carmel, clients follow a winding red-brick path through a garden to his studio, with its high and wide glass windows filled with the luminous canopy of curvy, fat-leaved oaks. Our home is surrounded by a venerable oak grove with several towering pines. This is another dollop of synchronistic magic. Oaks are prominently featured in mythology, evoking strong associations with the goddess Aphrodite, and the goddess Diana, my namesake, and the oaks are specially prized for their oracular power. During the process of selling our Sherman Oaks home, I would seek counsel with the trees in our back yard and beseech them to help us find a home equally verdant with their kind. They came through in flying colors with their ancient internet.

And here we have arrived, with deer families leaping across the front lawn and red-tailed hawks watching from gnarly high branches for meals in the ivy below. Raccoons scavenge with attitude. Somehow we've managed to establish ourselves amongst the same community of wildlife as we did in the Hollywood Hills, including the occasional spotting of a mountain lion. The resilience of wild creatures in maintaining their presence in our civilization gives me hope that any new mythology arising in our times might give testimony of the continuing presence of the untamed creatures of our inner and outer lives. Carmel chimes with such mythic, magical, and wild music.

What a far piece it has been, as I reflect on the paths traveled by the little girl with her years in an orphanage and with foster families on the east coast. My mother, so eager to be in Carmel where she had enjoyed several visits, passed away during our move here. That sadness I feel even now, and I've not yet been able to release her ashes to the Pacific. These reflections and memories of many happier moments of my childhood reveries have been bridged by all the dreams and improvisations leading from where I began to where I have been led by Eros—to my inevitable place and places. As a little girl I would look out the windows of that huge, institutional building, the orphanage, and wonder how I ever could climb those large mountains to make my way home. I recall Psyche's climb, her resilience. It seems my whole life I have followed where Eros has led me, where Eros was beheld, to *be held*. Home indeed seems to me to be all those inevitable places where Psyche and Eros perennially meet.

Honoring that showbiz admonition to exit the stage while the audience still appears to be alert, let me leave this bidding with you, dear Reader. I wonder how has it been for you thus far in your life, at whatever age and in whatever circumstances you find yourself today? How have you been following in your own life the Eros that Psyche is looking for, perhaps without always noticing?

WORKS CITED

Apuleius, Lucius. (Robert Graves Translation) *The Golden Ass*. New York: Farrar, Straus and Giroux, 1979.

Bolen, Jean Shinoda. *Goddesses In Everywoman*. New York: HarperCollins, 1984.

Campbell, Joseph, with Bill Moyers. *The Power of Myth*. New York: Doubleday, 1988.

DeCastillejo, Irene Claremont. *Knowing Woman: A Feminine Psychology*. Boston, MA: Shambhala, 1997.

Downing, Christine. *The Goddess: Mythological Images of the Feminine*. New York: Continuum, 1999.

Estes, Pinkola Clarissa. *Women Who Run With The Wolves*. New York: Ballentine Books, 1995.

Fox, Matthew and Sheldrake, Rupert. *Natural Grace*. New York: Doubleday, 1996.

Friday, Nancy. *The Power of Beauty*. New York: HarperCollins, 1996.

Hillman, James. *The Myth of Analysis*. Evanston, Illinois, Northwestern University Press, 1999.

Hooks, Bell. *Teaching to Transgress: Education as the Practice of Freedom*. New York: Routledge, 1994.

Houston, Jean. *The Search For The Beloved*. New York: Jeremy P. Tarcher, 1994.

Johnson, Robert A. *Lying With the Heavenly Woman: Understanding and Integrating the Feminine Archetypes into Men's Lives.* New York: HarperCollins, 1995.

Johnson, Robert A. *She: Understanding Feminine Psychology.* New York: HarperCollins, 1989.

Labouvie-Vief, Gisela. *Psyche and Eros: Mind and Gender In the Life Course.* New York: Cambridge University Press, 1994.

Murdock, Maureen. *The Heroine's Journey.* Boston, MA: Shambhala, 1990.

Neumann, Erich. *Amor and Psyche: The Psychic Development of the Feminine.* New York: Princeton University Press, 1971.

O'Donohue, John. *Anam Cara: A Book of Celtic Wisdom.* New York: Harper Collins, 1997.

Scott, Mary Hugh. *The Passion of Being Woman*, Denver, Colorado: MacMurray and Beck, 1998.

Shlain, Leonard. T*he Alphabet Versus the Goddess.* New York: Viking Penguin, 1998.

Swimme, Brian. *The Universe Is A Green Dragon.* Santa Fe, NM: Bear and Co. 1984.

Wilkinson, Tanya. *Medea's Folly.* Berkeley, CA: Page Mill Press, 1998.

Wolkstein, Diane. *The First Love Stories.* New York: HarperCollins, 1991.

ACKNOWLEDGMENTS

Many ants, reeds, eagles and towers, in other words, supportive and inspirational women and men, animals and landscapes helped shaped my life and this book. Much gratitude to:

Artist, poet Carolyn Mary Kleefeld: Touchstone to this myth and Carmel. Your exquisite prologue and painting on the cover, unique life and work, dazzle this myth to fullness in beauty, soul, and eros.

Artist and cherished friend Melanie Gendron: From youngest dreams shared, two young psyches spinning a long friendship, you continue to inspire with your art, humor and wisdom gleaned from leaning bravely into the deep.

Luminous actor, Ellen Burstyn: Special thanks for reading and endorsing a manuscript from a stranger. Your memoir, *Lessons On Becoming Myself*, is among the most riveting, revealing and uplifting I've ever read by a woman/actress.

Actor and dear friend, Barbara Babcock: Your curiosity, intelligence, beauty, talent, pluck and grace, deepen and illuminate my life, along with our profound love and concern for animals.

Professor Hendrika de Vries: Your encouragement to publish this book, your goddess and Psyche evoking presence teaching the myth of Psyche and Eros, revealed its transforming boons as nothing else had.

Poet and professor Peter Thabit Jones: Your support of this work, your stirring Welsh voice reading poetry amongst the Big Sur trees, cast whispers of light into my soul.

Scholar, poet, and editor John Dotson: The outstanding champion and tiller of this work, your strengths and soulful ear to this tale helped unfurl the powerful beauty ointment the feminine voice resonant in this myth holds for all women and men.

Acknowledgments

Beloved and gorgeous friends, Patricia and Norman Gaul-Kremer: A heart overflowing for your immense hearth of love and support given during my school years, and thereafter. Your friendship is among my life's most joyful and rewarding treasures.

Colleague, dear friend Esther Hutchison: Your unstinting support of my talents, your caring presence at a trying time, our fellow wayfaring adventures born from Eavesdroping on Mt Olympus have brought delight, depth and a soulful music.

Late friend and heavenly mentor Gabriele Weisshaar: I cannot imagine my life without the beauty of goodness, wisdom and spiritual heft you bequeathed to it, along with our bountiful connections to animals and nature. You are still my north star.

Late enchantress Laura Archera Huxley: Eros swirled through you and your home in the Hollywood Hills in a captivating mist. You continue to inspire me to live passionately, inquisitively, undaunted by time, singing to the end.

Entrepreneur at heart Gary McKinstry: So thankful for our childhood theatricals in your parent's barn in the Berkshires. And for the love and attention you gave to my mother.

Anthony Mauriello, for your generous heart and love, and for helping to ripen my young psyche to maturity.

Jungian therapist and friend, Susan McGuire, for laughter, wisdom and authenticity learned in the warmth of good times together.

Friend, Reverend Karen (Suddhi) Weingard, for sowing glittery seeds of bravery, daring, and flamboyant joy. Before Lady Gaga, there was you.

Kindred hearts, Haya and Jake Sakadjian, for championing my return to academia with your spirited, generous gifts.

Others to thank include: Stellar Professor/author Ginette Paris for ferrying me through the shoals of my doctoral dissertation; the Meyer family, Kristin, Michael, Hanna, and Lily for their affectionate and generous support of my midlife return to school; to Jennifer, Thor, Elie, Basil, and Jack Erickson for their boundless support, laughter, good food, good wine, and good times always with our beloved hounds; to lovely Patricia Holt for her big-hearted offerings on my behalf; to Kris Klute and, Ty Griffin for wise and guiding edits; for Professor Tanya Wilkinson for her enlightening assistance at the beginning; to all my outstanding and stimulating professors at the California Institute of Integral Studies, and the Pacifica Graduate Institute. And to Professor/visionary Lori Pye for the opportunity to teach Ecopsychology at The Viridis Graduate Institute.

Lovely Elizabeth Porter (Annie) of River Sanctuary Press: That this manuscript found its way to you with your editorial gifts, sensitivities to the material, and publishing experience, midwifing *Psyche, Eros, and Me* into the book I hoped it could be—I am so grateful, and for your generous, guiding light.

To my late mother: Your never-ending beauty, indomitable courage, intelligence, kindness, and concern for others, and most of all your love and enthusiastic spirit never cease to hold and nurture me. A loss for both of us—when you lost your voice. Thank you for helping me find mine.

To my remarkable, beloved husband Robert Edwards: The territory and travels of our years is vast with endless gifts to thank and love you for. You helped me find my deep singing self, as you have so many others, with kindness, dedication, and brilliance. Few teachers possess your caring nature and exceptional knowledge. You supported my return to school, and my acting days and dreams. Thank you for the beautiful, abundant life you helped provide for us, as we grew our souls and love through many years together.

Dearest canine beloveds: Shanti, Walker, Evie, Asher, Winnie and Calder: Happiness has been being with you, enmeshed in your scented fur, sandy beach paws, couch snuggles, perky intelligence, hilarious antics, and eyes of love. You are the rousing home for my animal soul.

And with reverence for Mother Earth and all her creatures. She who gave us ourselves and guided us all along.

New Releases from *River Sanctuary Publishing*

Adama Discourses: Walking the Light Path with Intention and Purpose, a channeled work by Ashalyn and Adama the Telosian, 2015. $23.95

Love, Alba (a novel), by former NY Times bestselling author Sophy Burnham, 2015. $15.95

My Mother—Myself: Glimpses into the Complicated Mother-Daughter Relationship, stories collected and edited by Bobbie Spivey, Billie Furuichi and Edy Henderson, 2015. $14.95

A Goddess Journal, (blank journal with illustrations and affirmations) by Melanie Gendron and Annie Elizabeth, 2015. $12.95

The Blue, a novel of romance, adventure and espionage, by William Sun, print and eBook 2015. $15.95

Other Favorites

Hands and Heart: Stories of General Surgery, by Michael DeHaan, 2013. $14.95

Mandalas for Therapy, Meditation and Fun! a coloring book by Lisa Cano, 2014. $15.95

River Sanctuary Publishing
P.O. Box 1561
Felton, California 95018
www.riversanctuarypublishing.com
(831) 335-7283

We offer custom book design and production with worldwide availability through print-on-demand, with personalized service and the most author-favorable terms in the industry. Specializing in inspirational, spiritual and self-help books, biography, and memoirs.

www.ingramcontent.com/pod-product-compliance
Lightning Source LLC
LaVergne TN
LVHW011425080426
835512LV00005B/276